Gabriele Bruehl

THE NEW TOWER OF BABEL

By the same author:

Liturgy and Personality
Transformation in Christ
Christian Ethics
and other works

THE NEW TOWER OF BABEL

Essays by

DIETRICH VON HILDEBRAND

Professor of Philosophy
Graduate School, Fordham University

P. J. KENEDY & SONS · NEW YORK

LIBRARY OF CONGRESS CATALOG CARD NUMBER 53-12221

PRINTED IN THE UNITED STATES OF AMERICA

TO MY

FORDHAM STUDENTS

CONTENTS

INTRODUCTION

"Interficere errorem; diligere errantem."—St. Augustine

In my youth I was acquainted with an old gentleman —an "original"—who was known to have a criticism for everything. As a matter of fact, every six months he moved from one country to another with his entire family and all his possessions, because after that length of time the place where he had been living seemed to him to be the worst on earth. Once I met him in Munich at a very beautiful concert in which a famous ensemble played Beethoven's Late Quartets. As this gentleman was a great music lover, I thought to myself: "This time he will find no grounds for criticism." But I was wrong. I found him raging and indignant. He said to me: "Isn't it a shame to see those four men sitting before us sweating, making so much effort and going through all that tension and anxiety while we enjoy and applaud the sight. It is nothing short of sadism. I cannot stand it any longer."

He gave a perfect description of how a given situation appears when we sever it from its real meaning and theme. In treating this musical performance as though it were silent and mute, in ignoring the music, the performance and its surroundings were distorted and made to seem ridiculous. This is precisely what happens when we look at the world as if God did not exist.

These essays are intended to examine various manifestations of escape from God in our present epoch. Of course every such escape is futile; in every period of history even those who try to deny God bear witness to His presence—analogous to the case of the skeptics who testify by their very denial to the existence of truth. Every attempt to ignore God shares the fate of the Tower of Babel.

Nevertheless, we are not thereby dispensed from the obligation to uncover all aspects of this escape from God and to denounce all tendencies toward secularization and rebellion against Christianity. Our God-given task is not to assume the role of passive spectator to the ruling of Providence in history, but to take a position with respect to events, to recognize dangers, and to combat those tendencies not in accord with the spirit of Christ. We must realize that God expects us to diagnose the mental diseases of our times, to warn of their dangers, to resist and fight them. We are not expected to divine the intention of Providence and to conform our attitude to what we suppose to be these intentions. Our concern must be to inquire whether a given trend or attitude is in its very nature right or wrong, whether or not it can stand the test before Christ. As soon as we uncover dangers we cannot but heed the call of God to unmask the wolf in sheep's clothing, to denounce errors, to trace them to their very roots, because it is only in striking at the roots that we can hope to overcome the evil.

We are fully aware of the impossibility of passing a global judgment on an historical era. There are so many different trends, movements, mentalities, in one and the same epoch, not only in different countries but in one and the same country, that the danger of oversimplification and unwarranted generalization becomes immense.

This danger of uniform interpretation remains even when we refrain from a global judgment and take into account the fact that in every historical epoch, individuals can be found whose lives furnish a contrast to the general spirit of the age. This applies *a fortiori* to judgments concerning the epoch in which we ourselves live. Progressive people, for whom the word "modern" is the highest encomium, tend to become ecstatic in praise of their own epoch. "Conservative" people, on the contrary, are inclined to think that everything was better in former times, that the very fact something is "modern" means that it is evil.

We are fully aware of the necessity of refraining from any global judgment on our times. Moreover, we want to emphasize at the start that the criticisms contained in the following articles carry with them no intention of denying the existence of many bright aspects of our epoch. As in all periods of history when terrible persecutions occur, we witness today a great and admirable heroism on the part of their victims. Our epoch is above all great because it has given rise to many martyrs and many secret saints. And even if we prescind from these manifestations of grace in the souls of the followers of Christ, our times are encouraging in other respects.

It is a period of specific contradiction. Concomitant

with the alarming and disastrous manifestations dealt with in this volume, we find great progress from the point of view of personalism in the enormous improvement in the condition of the working classes in democratic countries when compared with their status under nineteenth-century capitalism. This change shows an increasing respect for the dignity of the human person and a triumph of justice which should in no way be minimized.

Moreover, the very fact that in our epoch the impossibility of life without God—the attempt to escape from God—has reached its logical *reductio ad absurdum* shows a great and hopeful sign. Our epoch is more awake, more restless, more shaken, more apocalyptic, when compared with the complacency of the liberal era, with its humanitarian illusions of the possibility of living a happy and meaningful life without God. The vision of hell presented by the totalitarian states of Nazi Germany and Soviet Russia have drastically revealed the appearance of a world where an attempt has been made to stamp out all traces of Christianity. The illusion of a merely humanitarian paradise has been belied by these horrors.

Our period is great because it again teaches man the forgotten truth of which St. Peter speaks: "Be sober and watch: because your adversary the devil, as a roaring lion, goeth about seeking whom he may devour." (I Pet. 5:18)

The world picture offered by existentialist atheism is more consistent and illustrative than that of other forms of atheism. In its pessimism, in considering anxiety and concern as the basic human experiences, it is much more "true" than the unmotivated, superficial optimism of materialists and positivists.

There are more psychic diseases today; man suffers more from the meaninglessness of a world without God than ever before. The modern man thirsts for the absolute. Notwithstanding the symptoms of the dethronement of truth on which we shall insist in one of the following essays, there exist in many souls the thirst for truth and the restlessness of the search for truth.

In spite of the unprecedented Soviet anti-personalism—and widespread misconception of the person in democratic countries as well—there have been few periods in history in which the fight for certain basic rights of the human person has been carried on with such ardor and vigor. The dignity of the human person is written over this period as its objective theme, regardless of how few persons hold the right and valid notion of this dignity and its metaphysical basis. This epoch is great because the struggle that centers around the human person is ultimately a fight under the banner of Christ, even if this is not admitted by many of those who earnestly oppose Communism on different grounds.

Yet all that can be said in praise of our epoch makes it all the more necessary to raise one's voice and to combat the specific errors and perversions of our times. The greater our awareness of the importance of this hour, the better our understanding of the objective theme of this epoch, the greater is our responsibility to try to uncover that real theme, to attempt to expose those attitudes and trends that endanger its fulfillment.

The individual person is not a prey to an irresistible historical development in the sense of animals and plants in evolution: man is a free being who can and should stir the course of history by influencing the mentality of an epoch, its convictions, its approach to the world, according to his concept of the true and right. The role entrusted by God to the individual person, as a being capable of knowledge and endowed with a free will, to whom God has spoken, who has been called by Him, implies a tremendous responsibility.

Furthermore every man is exposed to an infection by the errors and perverted trends that are, as it were, in the air of an epoch. To become fully alive to these dangers and aberrations is, therefore, imperative also for our own sake.

Finally, the words of St. Paul should be our device: ". . . prove all things; hold fast that which is good" (I Thess. 5:21).

DIETRICH VON HILDEBRAND

New York
Octave of the Ascension, 1953

THE NEW TOWER OF BABEL

HUMANITY is at the crossroads. This is true whether we speak of the great debate between Communism and democracy, or of the entire spiritual situation.

The conflict between totalitarianism and democracy concerns the relation between the individual and the state. Totalitarianism claims an absolute sovereignty of the state over the individual, denies completely the rights of the person, who is conceived as nothing but a mere part of a collective entity; whereas democracy insists upon the inalienable rights of the individual and stresses the limits of state sovereignty according to natural law. This conflict, though a specifically drastic expression of the present crisis, is, however, but one aspect of the great decision at stake. In order to understand the entire impact of the crisis we have to dig deeper.

The real conflict is between Christianity on the one hand and a thoroughly anti-Christian conception of life on the other. This struggle has reached a decisive stage, has become a radical clash between two worlds, embracing all domains of life and human existence. The liberal age was an age of compromise. Notwithstanding its anticlericalism and its contention against Christian doctrine in the religious and philosophical fields, it retained Christian elements in the moral, sociological, juridical, and cultural spheres. Our present age, however, reveals a consistent, anti-Christian conception in every domain of life on the part of the enemies of Christianity.

The mark of the present crisis is man's attempt to free himself from his condition as a created being, to deny his metaphysical situation, to disengage himself from all bonds with anything greater than himself. Man endeavors to build a new Tower of Babel.

In his profound work, *The Drama of Atheist Humanism,* Père Henri de Lubac has analyzed the historical sources of this present crisis in Feuerbach, Nietzsche, Comte, and others. He exposes convincingly the dissolution of man brought about by the penetration of a consistent atheism into every domain of life. This dissolution finds its theoretical expression today in Heidegger's and Sartre's existentialism—the latter claiming to be a new and authentic humanism.

We need to become interested more in the real approach of modern man to life than in theories about it. We need to be more existential than Sartre in analyzing the different forms of a way of life in which the basic attitude of freeing ourselves from our condition of creatures finds its expression. We have to distinguish two main forms: first, the individualistic self-sufficiency as it is found in many Western democratic countries; second, the collective anti-personalism as it is represented by Communism.

The existentialism of Sartre is in certain respects a theoretical formulation of the basic attitude to be found in these two forms. Sartre says: *"L'homme n'est rien d'autre que ce qu'il se fait,"* and he declares this to be the first principle of existentialism. In order to understand the position of Sartre, we must realize that for the existentialists, existence precedes essence, and that the radically undetermined will is the source of existence. No object has an essence that imposes itself on man. It is exclusively what his approach makes it for him. Also, man himself has no nature that precedes his will. His nature is itself a result of his arbitrary will. There exists no good or evil that offers itself to our free choice. It is our arbitrary decision that makes a thing good by the very fact that we choose it.

Sartre's thesis implies a radical denial of the creaturely character of man, and as such it is a drastic theoretical expression of the attempt to build a new Tower of Babel, an endeavor we find at the base of individualistic self-sufficiency as well as of collectivistic anti-personalism. The chief stress will be laid here on this individualistic self-sufficiency, whose danger is less obvious than the vision of hell embodied in totalitarianism.

This individualistic self-sufficiency is characterized by the rejection of all bonds linking us to God and to moral law. The modern man who is affected by this perversion refuses to conform to the call of values, to surrender, to submit to something for its own sake, for the sake of its own intrinsic nobility and sublimity. Reverence, obedience, gratitude are alien to him. He does not want to abandon himself; on the contrary, everything becomes a means for his arbitrary pleasure and satisfaction. He looks upon marriage as something with which he can deal according to his arbitrary mood and not as a holy bond, something sublime that he is compelled to respect. He contracts marriages and gets divorces as he exchanges one glove for another. Instead of seeing in children a gift of God, he himself wants to determine their number by birth control. On the one hand, he believes himself entitled to shorten the lives of others and his own by euthanasia, when they seem to him no longer worth while; on the other, he wishes to become forgetful of death—the tragic, implacable tribute of our creaturehood—as is evidenced in the cemeteries of Los Angeles which Evelyn Waugh stigmatizes in his work *The Loved One*.

Further—and here we touch an especially important point—he no longer wants to admit the existence of that factor in our life as creatures which is often called "chance" and which a Christian calls Providence. He himself wants to determine everything; he seeks to replace the rhythm of a truly human life with its constant dependence upon factors that we cannot ourselves control—the element of surprise, of a gift bestowed upon us, of bliss and trial—with a human insurance against all the unforeseen and unforeseeable elements.[1] He wants to exclude by eugenics the possibility that men who are crippled or mentally deficient should have existence. He wants to exclude by human means the possibility of his having an unpleasant employer, of his depending upon the kindness and generosity of another

[1] This must not be understood as though we denied that man should use his talents in order to protect himself and to use all forces in nature for his welfare. But the success in this respect must never lead him to fall into the illusion of being no longer a creature. The domination of nature must never assume the character of replacing Providence. Above all, should we abstain from the attempt to subdue the sphere of higher goods in the same way, as they have by their very nature the character of a gift.

person.[2] He refuses to receive any gifts, but wants to claim everything as his right. He does not rejoice in experiencing the charity and generosity of his neighbors because these are factors which he has not himself determined and which call for gratitude.

He no longer approaches beauty in nature and art with reverence, as something reflecting a higher world above him. He treats beauty as something he relishes like a good wine. He makes no effort to seek beauty where it is, but wants it to be offered to him on a dish while he sits back and relaxes. He does not want to be raised above himself, to emerge from his own accustomed atmosphere, but he wants beauty to be drawn into his realm as mere fun or entertainment.

He wants to be himself the source of all authority in community life. His is no longer the conception of democracy which provides that the individual shall be free to determine the structure and the laws of community life according to the objective norms of right and wrong, in which freedom consists in the fact that one is called to co-operate in finding what is objectively right. His concept of democracy means rather that the majority arbitrarily decides what is right and wrong, that the arbitrary will of the individual is the very source of right and wrong. In other words, the arbitrary will

[2] Again, we have to emphasize that this criticism in no way implies that there should be no protection of elementary rights by social laws. The essential point is the clear distinction between the things which by their very nature call for regulation by the state and even for the eventual application of force—such as the protection of rights, and those which are by their very nature based on the spontaneity of the individual, and cannot be approached in juridical terms, and which forbid their enforcement by state laws.

of the individual replaces here the objective norm. Instead of believing that there is a chance that the majority of men will choose that which is objectively right, right independently of their will, this modern man believes that their arbitrary decision makes a law right and legitimate.

One of the most striking symptoms of the attempt to deny our creaturehood is betrayed in the position that many men take today toward knowledge.[3] Here we are confronted with a peculiar contradiction: on the one hand, the ordinary philosophy of relativism affirms as a self-evident fact that there is no objective truth. On the other hand, science is set up as a fetish. On the one hand, objective truth is radically denied; on the other, science is accepted as an undisputed authority. It seems as if the resentment against metaphysics has reached a stage of such violence that men are willing to accept everything as true from a teacher who has officially denied the possibility of attaining objective truth as such. Patently, the rebellion against truth is primarily a rebellion against philosophical truth, against truth in the field of ethics, of metaphysics, of epistemology. It is the hatred of absolute truth, culminating in the hatred of supernatural truth. Those who do so, however, do not realize that in denying objective truth in general, that in denying the validity of the first principles, they have undermined science as well. If there exists no objective

[3] Cf. "Dethronement of Truth," pp. 57 ff.

truth, if it is impossible to make any valid statement, science also is a meaningless, empty, intellectual game, and we can expect from science neither any solution to practical problems nor any information. The reasoning of these people seems to be based on a crass contradiction: that science has proved that there is no objective truth.

Another paradox is that never before has man placed so much trust in learning as in our time—a time when objective truth is ridiculed as an anachronism. Never was there such a hunger for learning, never before have so many people felt themselves frustrated if prevented from studying, never before did man believe that everything can be acquired by taking courses in a subject, and that studying is the chief and the surest way of gaining the ability to perform something well. Abilities based on special gifts, such as an understanding of art, are believed to be accessible to everyone by study.

In this adulation of learning, one forgets that there are many things that are pure gifts which we cannot acquire even with the greatest assiduity: they are endowments granted to us by God. To these gifts belong, for instance, creative artistic talents, as well as profound sensitivity to art, music, or literature, philosophical power, or scientific intuition.

One forgets, further, that even among those things that can be acquired, not all of them can be acquired by learning in the strict sense of the term. In the sense in which a language or ancient history or chemistry can be learned, not everything that can be acquired can be learned. The idolatry of learning is precisely characterized by this "rationalism" which assumes that there is nothing that could not be acquired by following certain courses in a subject.

Instead of understanding that in many domains the right knowledge is only a presupposition for achievement, one erroneously believes that neutral studying should suffice to fit him for any task and mission. Actually there are many tasks and missions whose fulfillment necessarily requires, over and above knowledge, the co-operation of the will, obedience, the inspiration of great examples, guidance by a moral authority, the influence of a pure and great atmosphere in the environment, and many other factors.

Again, this "rationalism" is so uncritical that its victim forgets that the authority of a university gives no guarantee that he receives true information, even concerning many of those things which, as such, really can be acquired by rational assimilation. Whereas in natural sciences, such as physics, chemistry, physiology, or astronomy, the authority of a university is a guarantee that the professor will transmit to his students ascertained results of scientific research, this in no way applies to philosophy. Here the truth of what is taught depends exclusively upon the question of who is the man teaching philosophy. The fact that he is a university professor in no way safeguards a man from being filled with stupid and erroneous ideas. The threefold error of believing, first, that everything can be acquired by our own powers; second, that the way to acquire anything is learning in the strict sense; third, that courses given by any professor at any university are an authentic source for knowledge of the subject we want to learn, gives to the passion for learning the character of an inane and naïve rationalism.

It is believed that activities the qualifications for which are primarily based on moral virtues and moral wisdom, such as personal advice and helping other persons in difficult situations, can be well performed through studying a textbook on sociology. To be a good father, a good spouse, is considered a lesson capable of being taught and learned through a course in psychology.

What in former times was believed to be the result of religious formation is now considered to be the result of taking courses in sociology. What presupposes a heroic dying to ourselves and abandonment to God is thought to be attainable by taking a degree. In general, it is believed that one can become an expert in every subject by attending courses in a college or university and by reading the respective textbooks. And it is thought that being an "expert" guarantees that one has a real, deep, intuitive relation to the realm studied, and enables one to perform any task well.

Man no longer understands that culture is based not only on knowledge, that in order to be a bearer of culture or to embody cultural values a person must possess many things which cannot be acquired by mere learning and which are, in part, even independent of a college education. An artisan of fifteenth-century Florence was certainly more cultured than many a university professor of today. True culture is a living part of a personality, and it is manifested in the way one views the universe, in the nature of the goods which play a role in one's life and which are one's spiritual nourishment, in the richness and genuineness of one's experiences. It is manifested, further, in the standard of a person's work, in his language, his demeanor, the atmosphere he radiates—an atmosphere determined by the spiritual world in which his mind and soul are at home.

It is typical of the fetishism of learning that the illiterate is considered as the prototype of the absence of culture. In truth, the illiterate can be the bearer of a high culture, and the man who has taken several degrees may be lacking in all culture.

Gratifying and valuable as it is that libraries give to everyone the opportunity of reading great and important books, it would be a disastrous illusion to believe that culture in all its manifold aspects could be replaced by libraries offering as much information as possible on every subject, or even by an encyclopedia of all knowledge.

The fetishism of learning does nothing to enhance the great and responsible mission of the teacher, especially of the teacher whose subject is related to man's destiny. On the contrary, by placing every subject on the same level, as something that can be acquired through courses and taking degrees, and by considering the degrees of university professor as guarantee of the intellectual and moral stature of the teacher, one minimizes the real mission of those who are called to teach truth. This noble mission is leveled down to the business of being an official of a university.

We must thus add the fetishism of learning to the

fetishism of science as a characteristic of our epoch. The modern man is a relativist who shuns the idea of objective truth, proud of his critical superiority over the naïve dogmatists of former times; and in the same breath he most uncritically expects everything to be accessible through learning and accepts everything taught by relativists as absolute truth. How can one account for this paradox?

In reality, these attitudes stem from one and the same source. Contradictory as they are when professed by one and the same person, they both testify to the old truth, that the man who turns away from God inevitably becomes the prey of an idol. The one who wants to shake off the sacred bond of absolute truth will inevitably fall into the web of the most naïve, uncritical, not to say superstitious, worship of unfounded opinions. He who shirks *episteme* will inevitably become a disciple of *doxa*.

In reality, it is the denial of man's condition as creature which is at the root of this making a panacea of science, learning, and study. The same mechanistic spirit maintaining that the ideal is to be found in being able to determine everything according to our arbitrary mood gives rise to the supplanting of all other factors by mere learning, to the superseding of all mysteries by scientific explanation.

The egocentric sovereignty the modern man arrogates to himself bans everything that has the character of coming from above, of imposing bonds upon us, and of calling for an adequate response. The modern man also shuns all the factors in life which are gifts, which he cannot grant to himself: they would remind him of his dependence upon something greater than himself and above himself. Thus truth in its implacable sovereignty, absolute truth that judges our reason instead of being judged by it,[4] is denied. But a flat rationalism goes hand in hand with this rebellion against truth. To make of learning a panacea means to eliminate all the factors not in our power. To consider everything that is taught as accessible to everyone is again a satisfaction for the modern man's claim to sovereignty. Moreover, this passion for learning is not rooted in a real thirst for truth, but in the desire to share in the progress of our epoch, and to place ourselves more and more in a position of sovereign independence. It has more the aspect of Bacon's *"scientia est potentia"* than of St. Augustine's *"Quid enim fortius desiderat anima, quam veritatem?"* (What does the soul yearn for more ardently than truth?) [5]

All these concrete examples reveal the same fundamental feature: the rejection of man's situation of a creature, the ignoring of his metaphysical situation; in other words, the illusion of a complete self-sufficiency on man's part.

Three main elements characterize this basic attitude. The first is the denial of any *religio,* any bond with something objective which calls for obedience and sub-

[4] St. Augustine, *De libero arbitrio,* II, 12.
[5] *Tract. 26 in Joannem,* 5.

mission, any respect for whatever has an authentic value, and above all the refusal to surrender to God, the ultimate source of all values. It is a disordered, distorted conception of freedom. Freedom no longer means the enjoyment of the ineffable privilege conceded to man by God, the privilege of being able to conform in a free act of will to God, His eternal law and His will, of being able to respond freely and adequately to every good possessing an authentic value; rather, it has become the possibility of following arbitrarily one's inclinations and tendencies.

The second element is an illusion of man's possessing unlimited possibilities of achieving everything by his own strength. This is linked to the superstition of an automatic progress of humanity, a superstition that survives, astonishingly enough, in spite of the decline of humanity which our present epoch clearly reveals in so many respects.[6] Modern man has lost the consciousness of being a creature which even the pagan possessed, and he lives in the illusion that by his own powers he can transform the world into a terrestrial paradise.

The third element of this attitude is its distorted conception of happiness—that is, the belief that man will attain happiness in the measure in which he is able to determine by himself everything in his life. Père de

[6] It must be said that this superstition is a heritage of the liberal age and is not to be found in the existentialist conception. Here we touch upon a typical difference between the ethos of the individualistic and of the existentialist self-sufficiency. In the existentialist ethos there is something pessimistic, tense, anti-bourgeois, pathetic; whereas the way of life of the individualistic modern man is optimistic, soothing, and somewhat bourgeois.

Lubac eloquently describes how man in these times rebels against God in order to give himself the illusion of possessing arbitrary sovereignty and unlimited plenitude. He quotes Dietrich Heinrich Kerler: "Even if it could be proved by mathematics that God exists, I do not want Him to exist, because He would set limits to my greatness." [7]

It is obvious that this approach to life is a basic perversion and illusion. Man is not a self-sufficient being. The true nature of man can be understood only when we grasp his metaphysical situation and his being ordered toward God. It is not by accident that antiquity never clearly grasped the nature of the human person. But even in Christian *philosophy* the nature of man and especially his character as a person has not yet been completely elaborated. There still remains a gap between revelation, religious experience, and the philosophical notion of *animal rationale*. From a philosophical point of view, we have not yet fully exploited the astounding fecundity of ideas offered to us by Revelation. We often accept the words of the Gospel as self-evident, without fully understanding their philosophical implications.

I shall try to indicate two fundamental facts, the knowledge of which cannot be dispensed with for a true understanding of man's nature: first, the transcendence of man; second, the gift character of happiness.

[7] *The Drama of Atheist Humanism*, trans. Edith M. Riley (New York, 1950), p. 27.

By transcendence I mean that, unlike a plant or an animal, man is not only ruled by a teleological movement, a tendency to unfold his entelechy, but that he is able to respond to something greater than himself, to interest himself in goods possessing an authentic value for their own sake. In fine, man is able to respond to God with adoration and love. The metaphysical situation of man is characterized by the great dialogue between man and God. Whether he admits it or not, God speaks to every man as He did to Adam: "Adam, where art thou?" Whether he knows it or not, God speaks to him in a manifold manner through the goods possessing an authentic value. Man can acquire his natural and supernatural perfection only in responding adequately to this call. But this inner movement must not be interpreted as an urge to acquire his own perfection. This interest in every true value and above all in God is not motivated by the immanent desire to find one's perfection, one's own good, but is engendered by the intrinsic goodness and importance of the true value and, eminently, by God's infinite goodness. Pascal had a presentiment of this fact when he said: *"L'homme surpasse infiniment l'homme."*

Man is able to grasp things greater than himself and to take interest in them for their own sake. This transcendence differs radically from the transcendence of the existentialists. Sartre denies that man is ordered toward God. He means by transcendence not the capacity to respond to God for His own sake, not man's capacity for fecundation by something greater than himself, but rather a capacity to build up the world arbitrarily.

Instead of the freedom to conform to the call of God through the values which exist independently of man, which impose an obligation on man whether he likes it or not, instead of the basic attitude of *religio,* Sartre's freedom means the arbitrary sovereignty of a being who is his own absolute master.

The true transcendence of man reveals simultaneously his character as a creature and his unique superiority with respect to all impersonal creatures. It reveals a characteristic in man's nature which is presupposed by grace and without which we could not grasp the true meaning of the words, "Whosoever shall lose his life, shall preserve it" (Luke 17:33).

It is evident that in denying his creaturely character, in disengaging himself from all obligations toward God and the world of values, modern man cuts himself off from all real plenitude. Precisely in refusing to transcend himself in the true sense of the term, in assuming a status of self-sufficiency, in giving himself the illusion of an unlimited plenitude, he becomes shallow and empty.

Moreover, he also destroys by that attitude all true happiness, even on earth. Here we touch upon the second element I mentioned above: the character of happiness. True happiness is essentially a gift, a surplus bestowed on us only when we grasp the true value of a good, and interest ourselves in it because of its intrinsic goodness and beauty.

The happiness that flows into our soul when we witness a generous act of forgiveness presupposes that we grasp its intrinsic value and respond to it for its own sake; it presupposes the consciousness of the importance this act has in itself. Should we take an interest in it only as a means of procuring happiness, we would not only approach it in a morally wrong way, but we would never even experience this happiness. One who would say, "I have heard that love is such a blissful experience; therefore, I want to fall in love in order to experience it," can never love, nor ever experience the bliss of love. Love implies the interest in another person for his own sake; it must be rooted in the consciousness of the *lovableness* of the other person, in the genuine abandonment to him, in the consciousness that he *deserves* love. Only when love has this character of an authentic value response will true happiness flow into the lover's soul as a superabundant gift.

If a person uses religion as a means to experience peace and harmony, he will never acquire that peace and harmony. Only if he submits to God because this attitude is due to God, only if he is exclusively concerned with God's infinite beauty and goodness, and abandons himself to God in loving and adoring Him for His own sake, will true happiness flow superabundantly into his soul, as a gratuitous gift.

Thus, true happiness presupposes the consciousness of the autonomous intrinsic value of the object; it presupposes the consciousness of man's obligation to respond to it; it excludes an attitude of arbitrary sovereignty.

True happiness is essentially something we cannot give to ourselves. The man who wishes to determine everything himself not only cuts himself off from all depth and mystery, from all plenitude, but also from *true happiness.* What would the love of a person mean to us if it depended upon our arbitrary will to create it, if we could determine it as we put on and off an electric light? The great bliss of a love we receive would thereby be desubstantialized and become shallow. The bliss of being loved implies necessarily the free movement of another person toward us, the confrontation with a true reality that is not the work of our own hands.

For man's true happiness, the consciousness of depending upon something not submitted to our arbitrary will is necessary. True happiness presupposes respect for God-given bonds as well as the continuous rhythm of hope, so typical of our *status viae,* of being surprised, of experiencing our receptivity. It presupposes our dependence upon factors which are not in the realm of our power and of which we cannot arbitrarily dispose; it presupposes being confronted with a stream of life greater than we are ourselves. In trying to deny this essential condition of a human creature *in statu viae,* in eliminating as much as possible the factor of surprise in our life, in discarding all risk, in refusing to transcend ourselves, in tending toward a life which has nothing unforeseen, in which the product of our arbitrary determination grins at us everywhere, we condemn ourselves to boredom without end. We destroy the colorful richness of human life, the charm of situations, all poetry, but, above all, the depth and dignity of life. Happiness, moreover, essentially presupposes the confrontation with reality, an autonomous reality.

Mere fictions, mere illusions cannot render us happy. A mere fiction of a beautiful flower means nothing to us; it has to be a real being, which, because of its *real* existence, delights us.[8] A fictitious saint cannot gladden us; the consciousness that such a person exists is required in order to delight us.

Now, our consciousness of an autonomous, extramental reality presupposes that it is something which does not depend upon our arbitrary will, which imposes itself on us, which compels us to conform to its immanent law. The higher the object ranks, the more it is withdrawn from our arbitrary will, and the more its reality imposes itself on us. In Sartre's "world," in which every object is such as we form it by our arbitrary freedom, and where no obligations issuing from the object exist, there is no room for authentic happiness. Paradoxical as it may seem, in this existentialist world there is no room for experience of any existence other than our own. Thus even the reality of our own person is radically impoverished. In granting existence only to

[8] The fact that "fictions" in art can be a source of happiness is no objection against our statement. In art, the term "fiction" has a completely different meaning. Although the "story" of Hamlet is a fiction and the *dramatis personae* do not exist in reality, the drama *Hamlet* really exists as a work of art. The analogous reality whose existence is required in order to gladden us is, in this case, the *reality* of the work of art, which, by virtue of its beauty, is a source of joy. Also here a mere fiction—that is, the fiction that a great work of art would exist—could never be a source of joy. The beauty of the work of art is, moreover, a *message* and reflection of a higher world that is eminently real. All this applies *a fortiori* to a creative artist. The "ideas" revealed to him in the artistic inspiration can make him happy because they are discoveries and not mere arbitrary fictions. Moreover, the creative process is gladdening because it implies the experience of being privileged to give birth to something real.

the creations of an arbitrary will, Sartre leaves no place for the reality of the deepest and most profound experiences in our own souls, such as blissful peace or luminous harmony, for they also have the character of something which we cannot give to ourselves. They are a gift from above, and their reality and enjoyment presuppose that we cannot produce them arbitrarily.

Thus we see into what sort of blind alley the unwillingness to accept his condition as creature leads the modern man. By living in an illusion of godlike self-sufficiency, by yielding to a disordered ideal of freedom, he cuts himself off from all the sources of true happiness. His life becomes mechanized, deprived of all depth, richness, and color. He imprisons himself in a shallow, endless boredom. Nothingness stares him in the face.

The desubstantialization resulting from the rejection of creaturehood affects especially the spiritual wealth of the universe. Things that transcend the world of physics, chemistry, and physiology are no longer taken as belonging to an autonomous reality, but they are all placed on the level of images, illusions, semblances, which are looked at as mere thrilling, subjective "experiences."

In the philosophy and science of the last hundred years we observe a widespread tendency to look at the world *à la baisse*. It is based on the tacit, unproved thesis that the lower something ranks metaphysically, the more serious and incontestable is its reality. Instincts such as hunger, thirst, the sexual impulse are considered to be indubitable, serious realities; whereas will, love, knowledge, are considered to be questionable realities whose true substance can be reduced to instinct. One attempts to interpret the meaningful spiritual acts of cognizance, understanding, meaning, and judging in terms of "association." One endeavors to reduce the sublime spiritual act of love to a mere sublimated sexual instinct; one tries to place free will on the same level with instinctive desires. For these philosophers, lower beings have become the *pièce de résistance* of reality.

All spiritual entities are considered as mere by-products possessing no serious claim to full reality; they are approached with the categories proper to lower beings, which are taken as the *causa exemplaris* of the higher.

It is not our intent here to discuss the falsity of these dogmatic presuppositions, which no one has ever taken the trouble of trying to prove. What interests us is the fact that this prejudice has become an existential attitude, influencing many people's lived approach to being. For many it has distorted the authentic face of the world and of life.

It is especially the denial of the objective reality of values and their reduction to something merely subjective which become such a lived, existential *Weltanschauung*. Objective reality becomes humdrum; above all, it is stripped of its qualitative values.

The beauty of nature—that deep, meaningful voice,

that objective message of a higher reality than the one dealt with in science—the fascinating rhythm of history revealed in a great moment and situation, the specific atmosphere and pervading charm of a country, the impact of decisive and deep moments with a beloved person, the mystery in the relation between man and woman—all these things are no longer experienced as realities embracing us, as the *real* world in which we live and move, but as mere subjective impressions, nay, even as "fun." Man no longer believes in this full, dramatic reality, but he regards it as a romantic, subjective illusion which he can summon at his will, and which he can adapt to his arbitrary mood. It is dealt with as if it were on the same level as the hilarity which is an effect of alcoholic beverages, and which can be attained whenever we wish it. Man is thus no longer formed by the reality of these things but remains a dull spectator; he never pierces through his own triviality.

The mysterious spiritual "song" of every being endowed with authentic values, its qualitative plenitude, is no longer considered as an objective reality. The victims of this perversion then live and move in a colorless, gray, humdrum world in which only those things count which can be brought within practical or scientific categories, a world in which all mysteries—not only the supernatural but also all natural mysteries—are eliminated and ousted. The objective reality of all things is reduced to a blunt factuality. The atmosphere of a hospital waiting room or of a business office is looked upon as the authentic aspect of the world, the pattern of reality.

Yet all these spiritual factors not only bestow color, charm, meaning, depth, plenitude, dramatic rhythm, upon the "space" in which our life unfolds itself; they are also essential features of the universe. All the values embodied in created goods testify to the existence of a world above us and reveal the luminous beauty and mysterious depth which also *this* earth possesses, notwithstanding its being a "valley of tears." If the messages of God which are embodied in creation and which, as it were, make of the earth the *atrium* of the incomparably higher world of ultimate reality above us, are considered as merely subjective impressions, as romantic dreams, then the world would offer no reason whatsoever for joy and happiness. The emptiness and flatness, the meaninglessness, the insipidity of such a world, could engender only an endless metaphysical boredom, and ultimately despair. From this metaphysical boredom and despair no continuous entertainment by mere subjective illusions, semblances, and aspects could ever liberate us.

If the beauty in nature, the mysterious plenitude of interpersonal situations, the intense atmosphere of historical events, the spiritual frame of a nation and all the innumerable manifestations of its genius, are not objective, autonomous, vaild realities but mere romantic illusions, subjective semblances which do not call for responses, which are no longer taken seriously and respected in their reality, then they cannot elevate and enrich our life; they are flattened; they become a one-dimensional sight as in a panopticum or, in the best of cases, in a movie, merely able to entertain us for a while.

A typical manifestation of the desubstantialization of these spiritual entities, of their reality and depth, is the "reporter's" attitude toward every happening. The reporter views as objects of mere curiosity even the most dramatic happenings and the most intimate personal events that demand an approach antithetic to that of a spectator. By photographing a woman in tears over the death of her child, or by interviewing a person in the moment of parting from a loved one, one desubstantializes the situation and takes away its full human "thematicity," pressing everything down to a uniform low level.

The situation or the event then loses its impact of reality and its qualitative depth; one no longer lives *in* it, but it becomes a show, an example among thousands of others; one looks at it from without. Moreover, when the privacy and intimacy of life are destroyed, the depth, validity, and reality of most important experiences vanish.

There are essential conditions for validly experiencing the reality of spiritual entities, that is, conditions for a truly human life, a life capable of being fecundated and formed by all the spiritual richness of the universe and by the irradiation of the values embodied in it. As I have pointed out,[9] when discussing the virtue of *discretio,* every great and valid happening

[9] *Liturgy and Personality* (New York, 1943), chap. 8.

has its God-given rhythm in time, and by speeding up this rhythm arbitrarily we deprive the happening of its depth and genuineness, sometimes even of its validity. This God-given rhythm, indispensable for the development of a deep relation among persons as well as for the foundation of a religious order, for the creation of a work of art as well as for a philosophical work, is also an essential condition for experiencing the reality of values and of these spiritual entities. It is a part of *religio,* of our reverent attitude as creatures.

Another essential condition for a truly human life is that one must remain a full partner in the dialogue with all the spiritual messages of created goods, and not shift to an attitude of mere spectator looking at the situation from without. And the aforementioned "reporter attitude" is precisely incompatible with man's remaining a full partner.

If in a theater we are disturbed by the audience and deprived of the artistic illusion of the stage, our experience of the drama is frustrated. We are no longer embraced by the world of the drama, but we fall back into the social atmosphere of the theater. Analogously, the spell of any dramatic situation in life is destroyed as soon as we have placed ourselves outside it and assist as mere onlookers. Yet there exists a great difference between the two cases. In leaving the frame of artistic illusion in the theater, the frustration consists in being drawn out of the artistic illusion; whereas in the other case we are drawn out of the spell of the more authentic and valid reality, and thrown into a blunt, superficial, less authentic reality. Nonetheless, the analogy helps us to throw into relief the difference between being a partner and being a mere onlooker.

The reporter attitude, moreover, desubstantializes human life in still many other respects—i.e., by being antithetic to other essential conditions. To be bared before the public is fatal for all deep things that belong to the intimate sphere of the person. In order to understand this we must clarify the meaning of "public" in this context.

There exists a public sphere to which the liturgy refers when it says, *"Quidquid latet apparebit"* (All that's hidden shall be plain). In this holy public sphere of eternity there exists no disparity between its all-embracing public character and the most intimate "cell" of the soul. This coincidence is closely linked to the fact that Christ is the great secret of each soul and simultaneously the absolute common theme of all. On earth this glorious public sphere is to be found in the Holy Church alone, in the Corpus Christi Mysticum, in which the end of every individual soul and the end of the community converge into one. This sublime public sphere, far from depriving an intimate experience of its depth and secrecy, elevates it and gives it a new impact.

There exists, further, a terrestrial public sphere which is proper to great historical events, to important state affairs and decisions: a public sphere possessing dignity and solemnity. Yet this sphere is incompatible with intimate personal things. It can, by its very essence, embrace only things that are in their nature congenial to it. No attempt to draw intimate personal affairs into the public domain would ever mean incorporating them in this public sphere of history. It would mean, on the contrary, drawing them into a completely different kind of public sphere, the public "space" of publicity. Intimate personal things can reach into the public space of history only if, besides their personal meaning, they have assumed a historical impact, such as had the love of Antonius for Cleopatra, or the conversion of Clovis. Yet in these cases the private, intimate sphere is not abandoned, but since apart from their private personal meaning these facts have a historical content, they also reach into the historical sphere. Both spheres are thus not merged, but one and the same fact is incorporated in both spheres because of its twofold aspect.

As soon, however, as one attempts to draw into the public sphere something intimate that has no historical content, it is drawn only into the flat and trivial sphere of publicity, the sphere of advertising and scandal trials. This headline publicity is fatal to all great and deep intimate things; it desubstantializes them, empties them, profanes them. This publicity, food for sensational curiosity, razes the walls protecting the garden in which alone a deep human life can display itself as something real and valid.

Now, the reporter's attitude precisely draws everything into this sensational publicity and thus strangles the experience of full reality.

A third condition for a fully human life is to experience the uniqueness of important and profound events.

Though many things are happening every day and every hour all over the earth, such as marriage, death, childbirth, great sorrow, deep happiness, yet they have the character of uniqueness in the life of each individual. Shakespeare illustrates this fact in *Hamlet:*

> *Queen:* Thou know'st 'tis common;
> all that lives must die,
> Passing through nature to eternity.
> *Hamlet:* Ay, madam, it is common.
> *Queen:* If it be,—
> Why seems it so particular with thee?
> *Hamlet:* Seems, madam! nay, it is . . .

Every man is unique, and the greater and fuller a man's personality, the more unique he is. The birth of every child is a unique event, every great love, every death, and, above all, every baptism is unique. We cannot do justice to this unique and individual character of every great human event if we approach the world with a statistician's mentality. Man is able to grasp the uniqueness of all these great events only in the frame of his own life, a frame embracing also the beloved persons who are, as it were, the spiritual pillars of his life.

The individual who believes that *his* wedding is a unique event, that the birth of *his* child is as unique as if there never had been another birth before, is not falling prey to an understandable illusion. On the contrary, this aspect of uniqueness is the true aspect of these events in contradistinction to the one of statistics. Surprising as it may be, the uniqueness of the individual case cannot be understood unless the general character of such a classical human event is grasped. The more we see birth in the light of the words of our Lord: "But when she has brought forth the child, she remembereth no more the anguish, for joy that a man is born into the world" (John 16:20), the more we experience the uniqueness of the individual case. In the experience of the full reality and authentic impact of an event, the uniqueness of this individual happening and its general character of something classically and typically human interpenetrate each other. This interpenetration is revealed in the words of Faust in Goethe's drama: *"Der ganzen Menschheit Jammer fasst mich an"* (The misery of all mankind holds me in its grip).[10] Such are the words of the liturgy:

> A voice was heard in Rama, lamentation and great mourning; Rachel bewailing her children and would not be comforted because they are not (Matt. 2:18).

The character of individual uniqueness, which is closely linked to the depth and plenitude of the supra-individual essence, is incompatible with the statistical view, in which every individual is seen in the light of being a mere example of an average rule. The statistical approach deals with things having a deeply spiritual meaning and content in a way modeled after the pattern of material things and of happenings deprived of any deeper content, in which cases individuality does not have the same meaning and character as in the spiritual sphere. Such treatment is the very same reduction of the universe to blunt factuality which we mentioned above.

[10] *Faust,* Part I, last scene.

When we realize that the character of uniqueness of great things in human life goes hand in hand with the grand view of their general meaning *in conspectu Dei,* we have already avoided confusing this uniqueness with a ridiculous self-centered illusion that every event and every experience in our *own* life is incomparably higher and more important than are the analogous events and experiences in the lives of other persons. There are indeed many persons who fall prey to the silly illusion that *their* love is so exceptional that no other love can be compared with it, that *their* child is more beautiful, more intelligent than any other, and so on. The same people also are inclined to think that the headache that they feel is something absolutely uncommon, more intense than that of the others, or having a peculiar quality that they believe no one to have experienced before.

This illusion not only differs clearly from the experience of the uniqueness of classical human events, but even contradicts it. It is, first, incompatible with the grand view of the general meaning and nature of an event *in conspectu Dei,* which, as we saw, is essential for the experience of the real uniqueness. In its petty self-centeredness it radically excludes the wide, all-embracing nature of this view. Second, it contradicts the true experience of uniqueness because shutting ourselves up in our pettiness undermines all true, deep, classical experience. Pride and stupidity necessarily cut us off from the objective *logos* of being and from all values.

The true experience of the uniqueness of the great

human experiences in every individual case is, on the contrary, indissolubly linked with deference for these experiences in the life of one's neighbor. The love of neighbor is always directed to a concrete individual person, and not to mankind as such. This love is, furthermore, fully aware of the uniqueness of one's neighbor and never looks at him as a mere "case" in a series.

Analogously, the man who fully experiences the uniqueness of deep human events will regard these things with respect in the life of any concrete "neighbor" and will grant him that they are unique indeed. This view patently differs from the statistical view in which one sees these events as anonymous cases.

Yet there *should* be a difference between the meaning of these events in our own life and in the life of others. When things take place in the frame of our individual life, we are confronted with a message of God addressed to *us* in a specific way. This belongs to the very nature of our human structure and corresponds to a God-given order. It is obvious that a man's own marriage has another kind of uniqueness for him than the marriage of another person, that the birth of *his* own child is a specific message addressed to him and not to any other person. It is clear that the death of the one whom *he* loves is *his* cross and not his neighbor's. In the same way, it is absolutely right that the first smile of his child seems to be something unique to him and that it embodies for him the charm of a smile and of an awakening human being as such. The fact that the events of the same type are unique for every person to whose life they belong frustrates neither the "wideness" nor the "openness" for all that concerns other men, provided that everything is rooted in God and is incorporated in our relation to God, in the *religio*.

To conclude, uniqueness belongs essentially to the full reality of an important and deep experience. To approach it with the mentality of a statistician, as a mere case among others, desubstantializes it, silences its "song" and the reality of its value and meaning.

Great as the difference between a reporter's and a statistician's approach may be, they have in common the feature of desubstantializing the uniqueness of a happening. The reporter's approach leads to an even greater violation of the uniqueness and dignity of great experiences than does the statistician's cool, scientific approach. The reporter levels situations and events down to the plane of things that may attract our curiosity and our craving for sensation. His attitude is pregnant with the unrest proper to a continual turning from one case to another; he interprets all experiences by using the same categories, and implicitly denies their uniqueness. Now we can clearly see why this reporter's attitude, the atmosphere it conveys, the rhythm it introduces into life, frustrates man's experience of spiritual entities as objective realities and destroys the depth, quality, and dignity of human life.

A further essential pre-condition for experiencing the reality of spiritual things and for the full reality of our experiences is a rhythm of life which provides for periods of silence and solitude. How worn out and emptied do we feel on days when we have spoken too much, or in which there has been no moment of recollection. As I have pointed out in another book,[11] only a life in which recollection and contemplation have a place can be deep and valid. Without recollection, without this "coming to ourselves," which implies that we emerge from our actual occupations to the very meaning of our existence *in conspectu Dei,* we remain in the periphery and, as it were, the deep events and happenings cannot become full realities for us. They file before our eyes like television. We are not able to assimilate them, they cannot embrace us in their reality, but rather glide from us as water from a body smeared with oil.

Silence and recollection—apart from their fundamental importance in other respects—are also indispensable conditions for experiencing the reality of spiritual entities embodied in an event or a situation. The reporter attitude is the antithesis to the contemplative rhythm. It is a running from one event to another, it is the spreading of a raucous and typically unrecollected atmosphere; it snatches at the most intimate things that call for silence and contemplation and hurls them into the noisy, breathless, restless world.

Closely linked with this approach that desubstantializes the reality of higher goods is the failure to understand the meaning and function of forms. The classical meaning of exterior forms, as expressions of both our private and public life, is no longer understood. In the

[11] *Transformation in Christ* (New York, 1948), chap. 6.

liturgy we find the *causa exemplaris* of this meaning and mission of exterior forms. The position of the monks in the choir, the gestures of the priest during Holy Mass, the genuflection and the crossing of hands or extending of one's arms—all this eloquently testifies to the seriousness and intrinsic meaning of exterior forms.

Analogously exterior forms have a serious and genuine function in man's secular life. In former times, the validity and meaningfulness of adequate forms were fully understood, and found their expression in man's demeanor, in clothes, in innumerable customs, in private and social life, and in the rite of public actions. Today, our pragmatic attitude toward all those spiritual entities is such that exterior forms are no longer taken seriously. They appear as empty and ridiculous conventions or as vestments that no longer fit us; thus one tends to discard them. On certain occasions, one accepts them as a kind of amusing masquerade, or as a thrilling theatrical performance.

The withering of the sense for the meaning and value of forms has a twofold source. First, it is determined by the aforementioned stripping reality of its spiritual content, of its qualitative plenitude, and especially of its qualitative values. Form in general is typical of the spiritual and qualitative as opposed to the shapeless, potential, chaotic. The more form a thing possesses, the more definite and univocal is its face, the richer is its quality. This feature of form in general also extends to exterior forms of things, situations, and life. When experiences, situations, functions find an adequate expression in visible forms, the human "space" in which our life displays itself is rendered qualitatively richer and more colorful, because the reality of spiritual entities is more tangibly evinced and more easily experienced. The more the exterior forms disappear and yield to a uniform dullness or to a chaotic self-indulgence, the less the reality of spiritual entities is manifested, the less can it shelter us in its autonomous objectivity.

The second root of the vanishing of the sense of form is that man is no longer aware of his role as a creature. There exists a deep link between the meaning of exterior forms and the role that God has assigned to man on the stage of human existence. The inner forms of our life *in statu viae,* implying the *habitare secum* and opposed to all kinds of self-indulgence, call for adequate exterior forms.

In the clear confrontation of man with God as we find it in the liturgy, the twofold meaning of exterior forms of our external life is disclosed: the significance of a harmony between the inner life, such as should prevail according to God's will, and our own demeanor.

In the modern approach to life we are confronted with a striking paradox: on the one hand, man refuses to accept his condition as creature, he shirks submission to God and makes himself an absolute center; and, on the other, man no longer considers himself to be the lord of creation, as he is according to the Bible. The universe is viewed in the light of modern science and man is considered to be merely a more highly developed animal, set down and lost in this immense universe, inhabiting this secondary, small planet we call earth. On the one hand, man is conceived as a superman, unlimited in his evolution, capable of dominating nature more and more, capable of changing the "valley of tears" into a terrestrial paradise, or possibly even of prolonging human life indefinitely. On the other, one denies man's spiritual nature, his capacity for objective knowledge, his free will. His life is conceived as a result of physiological processes: love and happiness are believed to be determined primarily by glands.

From a rational point of view, these two approaches are clearly contradictory, but they ultimately derive from one and the same perversion.

When the world above us is denied, when all spiritual entities having the character of a gift are no longer considered as realities, when man no longer acknowledges his God-given destiny, when, on the contrary, he considers his life to be a by-product of physiological processes, then the attempt to determine everything more and more, and to change through natural science both our life and our condition on earth, is indeed a psychologically understandable illusion. But it is a tragic illusion, because by this desubstantialization of the universe, and by our blindness toward the reality of all spiritual entities and all mysteries, we banish also the possibility of true happiness already on earth. The reduction of the world to a gray materialistic universe on one hand and to a series of subjective impressions on the other condemns man to absolute boredom, eliminates all depth, all plenitude, all light, from human life.

Only the man who remains in the attitude of *religio*, who grasps the full objective reality of the spiritual entities reflecting the absolute reality of a world above us, filling our soul with longing and containing a tacit promise, only the man who aspires to be a servant of God, can understand the real lordship of man in this universe. Only he can grasp the organic, meaningful structure of the cosmos and his God-given role in it: "To serve God is to reign" (Postcommunion, Mass for Peace).

Let us state that it would be a great error to characterize this perversion of the modern man as paganism. Certainly the pagan world of antiquity had not yet a clear conception of God, of creation, or still less a consciousness of a need for *divine* redemption. The pagan Greek or Roman approached life *de facto* as a creature, conscious of his very dependence upon factors which he could not control. He even lived thoroughly in the attitude of *religio*. In Plato's *Phaedo* Socrates says when speaking about self-murder: "Yet I, too, believe that the gods are our guardians and that we men are a possession of theirs." [12] And the Platonic ideal of happiness is ecstasy, a being exalted above ourselves by something greater than we are. The pagan man shared neither in the superstition of an unlimited automatic progress nor in the ideal of discarding all bonds, of determining everything by his arbitrary will. He was reverent, and

[12] Trans. by Benjamin Jowett (New York, 1937), V, 445.

conscious of his dependence upon something above himself. The spiritual content of many high goods was experienced as reality; the "song" of things endowed with values was heard. We have to realize further that genuine paganism is impossible today, in the frame of our civilization. The "advent" position of humanity cannot be re-established. The approach to life which was possible before Christ can no longer exist today. Apostates differ essentially from pagans. In our modern civilization, with its highly developed technique, the naïve approach of the pagan can no longer subsist. The naïve *religio* of a primitive tribe and the natural *religio* of the ancients with their high culture are impossible for the modern man acquainted with our civilization. *Only in Christ* can the modern man reacquire the genuine life of a creature penetrated by *religio*. The lower status of the natural attitude of the pagan is no longer accessible to him. A grown-up person can never reacquire the natural simplicity and innocence of a child; in order to become like a child, according to the words of our Lord, he must be reborn in Christ, and this means achieving infinitely more than the natural simplicity of the child.

Even the relative genuineness and soundness of a truly human existence such as the pagan possessed can be acquired today only *per eminentiam,* on an incomparably higher level; it can be found only in Christ and through Christ. It goes without saying that the pagan attitude is equally in need of redemption. Every man, whatever his natural attitude, is menaced by a mysterious rupture and disharmony and can attain his eternal end only through Christ. But there exist, nevertheless, different degrees of perversion in the frame of the natural attitude itself.

Granted that this denial of the state of creature is a dangerous trend in the free world of today, the collectivistic form is a terrible reality in Soviet Russia and its satellites. Here the denial of creaturehood is embodied in a system. The state reserves to itself the role of playing God, and treats its subjects as though they were impersonal creatures.

We must distinguish between totalitarianism as such, which stems from terrestial messianism, and the Marxist-materialistic type of totalitarian state which is to be found in Soviet Russia. Or, in other words, we must distinguish between totalitarianism as a formal principle and the specific material end that the totalitarian state strives to realize in a concrete case. In Marxist Soviet Russia, the end embodies an outspoken *ressentiment* idol, based on a hatred of Christ and a consistent antipersonalism. Soviet Russia thus embodies the rebellion against God both in being totalitarian and insofar as its specific ethos and its end are concerned. In this context we shall stress primarily the totalitarian character as such.

The collective or institutional form as contrasted with the individualistic form is characterized by its belief that laws of the state can bring about a terrestrial paradise, that justice and absolute harmony can be brought to humanity by the right kind of constitution and laws. The conversion of the individual has become superfluous. The state is to take care of everything; that which is essentially a fruit of charity, generosity, and humility of the individual is to be enforced by the state—i.e., from without. Again we encounter the illusion that man needs no redemption, that by human means he can render life harmonious, just, and happy. But in contradistinction to the individualistic type, the collectivist expects everything from the intervention of the state. He replaces the religious and moral obligations that appeal to the free will of the individual with laws enforced by the state. Though it issues from the same roots as the individualistic form, the collective is incomparably worse. The mechanization and depersonalization of life is no longer a matter of aberration on the individual's part. It is withdrawn from his choice. It is brutally enforced upon him. He has no possibility whatsoever of opposing it or of fighting it.

The totalitarian state—and if it is to replace Providence it has no choice but to be totalitarian—leaves no place whatever to the deployment of a truly personal life; it rules every movement of the individual, his family life, his cultural activities, the frame of his possibilities, the degree and nature of his knowledge. It tends to deprive the life of the individual of every occasion for generosity, charity, or sacrifice. The religious spontaneously renounces his right to the use of private property: St. Francis distributed everything to the poor; the communist state forcibly deprives everyone of property—except the small group of party bosses. It consistently eliminates the occasion for generosity. It is obvious that in this terrestrial "paradise" there exists neither unforeseen good luck nor bad luck; there is no room for surprise, no rhythm of a truly colorful human life. The previously mentioned boredom is here replaced by a dreary, hopeless atmosphere, by a life sealed by fear and despair. Indeed, every attempt to create a terrestrial paradise without Christ, without the spontaneous co-operation of the individual with grace, must end in a Gestapo or a G.P.U. state.

The evil root of totalitarianism—the refusal to accept our condition as creatures—is the same as in the individualistic form, but now the collective entity has been substituted for the individual. The collective entity denies every bond toward God and His law; it shows the same arbitrary sovereignty at which the individual aims in the individualistic form. The achievements of this collective entity show the same shallowness, and though imposed by force on the individual, they lack the dignity and plenitude of something greater than the individual.

The *reductio ad absurdum* of the self-sufficiency of man becomes evident. The man who wants to be an absolute master, who renounces obedience to God, who believes himself able to create by his own forces a state of absolute harmony without Christ, makes of this world a hell, enslaves himself, and ends in a radical antipersonalism. Again we may quote Père de Lubac, who says, in his analysis of Comte's positivism: ". . . in founding his priesthood, he established the harshest and at the same time the most unjustifiable of intellectual tyrannies." [13]

Our real crisis, our authentic decision, is not between the individualistic form and the collectivist form, both denying our existence as a creature, both consistently atheist. It is the choice between a truly human life in the sense of *humanisme intégral,* on the one hand, and the secularized attitude of man who lives in the illusion of an absolute sovereignty on the other. It is the choice between a world without Christ and the world which has been redeemed by Christ, and in which everything is approached in the light of Christ.

In the truly human life based on the condition of man's existence as a creature the freedom of the individual is conceived as the possibility of a full unfolding of his personality, and an uncurtailed possibility of conforming to God, to His law, to the call of the true values. A truly human life is pervaded by an attitude of *religio,* by the consciousness that "God made us and not we ourselves" (Ps. 99:3).

It is a life framed by obligations, a life pervaded by the consciousness that every good possessing an authentic value calls for an adequate response and that it is not up to our arbitrary pleasure whether we respond to it adequately or not; a life in which we accept the gifts of God in a disposition of gratitude, realizing the obligations resulting from any true gift, the obligation to appreciate it, to protect it, to make sacrifices for its preservation.

[13] *Op. cit.,* p. 147.

To lead a truly human life implies an understanding that our existence is not based upon a sovereign display of our arbitrary moods, of a self-sufficient plenitude, but upon a free co-operation with the natural and supernatural gifts of God, upon the great dialogue with a reality independent of ourselves, upon transcending the realm of our own limited being, upon participating in God's infinite plenitude.

Truly human life further means the acceptance of our absolute dependence upon God, of a life with all its natural insecurity, risks, and sacrifices, in which we have to rely on Providence and not on our own forces and an automatic progress of humanity; a life in which ultimate bliss and success always remain a gift of God, however great our own efforts may be. As St. Paul expressed it, "I have planted, Apollo watered, but God gave the increase" (I Cor. 3:6–7). It means a life pervaded by the consciousness that "My times are in Thy hands" (Ps. 30:15). And concerning the person's relations to the state, it means the understanding of the limits of what state laws can effect.

Of course, the Catholic conception of life is not a pietistic and quietistic one, an attitude of indifference toward the *res publica* and of exclusive concern with our souls. Christ must also be the Lord of the earthly public sphere; the face of the earth should bear the seal of Christ, not only in the souls of the individuals, but also in the structure of the state and its laws. Yet the seal of Christ can be fully impressed on the state only to the extent that the Christian spirit lives in the individual members of the state and irradiates through them into the state. The perfectly just state presupposes the charity of the individuals within that state, and, above all, the free and spontaneous responses of the individual person are not only an indispensable presupposition for imbuing community life with the spirit of Christ, but they are as such more precious and important than any perfect law or institution could ever be.

Thus, the Christian does not expect the decisive change to come from the laws of a perfect state, but from the conversion of the individual. In grasping clearly the mission of the state and distinguishing the things which by their very nature have to be regulated by the state and imposed by state authority, from the things that can be contributed only by the spontaneous effort of the individual, the Christian will insist upon the inalienable rights of the individual and fight with all possible energy against any totalitarian conception.

It would be sheer nonsense to argue that, because we find germs of the individualistic egocentrism in many democratic countries, they do not have the right to fight the totalitarians and to claim that this fight is a struggle for the dignity of man. Despite the fact that trends revealing a rejection of creaturehood can also be found in democratic countries, nevertheless, the conflict between democracy and totalitarianism is *objectively* a struggle to prevent the world from being forcibly drawn into a denial of creaturehood and a demoniacal replacement of *religio* by a slavish submission to a deified state.

The great issue of this fight is to guarantee to man the

freedom of decision. It is the good fight, and its stakes also involve the preservation of those forces that will make it possible to fight with purely spiritual means for Christ.

The threat of Soviet Russia, which besides the horror of totalitarianism embodies a complete materialism and a flagrant anti-Christianity, must be opposed by military strength and full preparedness. Compelling as our duty is to stop this worst of enslavements of humanity and clearly as we must realize the grave and lofty mission entrusted to the United States to save the world from this unspeakable danger, the ultimate decision for humanity, the crossroads at which humanity stands today, implies more than the victory over Communism. It implies emerging from the "overdimensioning" of our human existence and overcoming the attempt to reject our situation as creatures. It implies a full conversion to Christ.

THE DETHRONEMENT OF TRUTH

One of the most ominous features of the present epoch is undoubtedly the dethronement of truth. In former times, whatever might have been professed, doctrines were always put forward with the claim that they were true. All theories, however erroneous and absurd their content might have been, appealed always to the question of truth as to the ultimate, decisive judge. From the very beginning of our occidental culture, all errors were propagated in the name of truth. The question of whether something was true or not was taken very seriously, and even when the real motives for adhering to an error were unconsciously rooted in the will of the erring person, truth was acknowledged to be the supreme, ultimate judge of every theory.

Paradoxical as it may seem, even the various theories that denied objective truth or the possibility of knowing it, such as skepticism, relativism, agnosticism, were advanced in the name of truth. Lengthy books were written in order to prove that the denial of truth was irrefutable from the viewpoint of truth. No one hesitated to recognize truth as the ultimate judge, in spite of the fact that the proposed thesis denied objective truth. In denying truth, man appealed implicitly to truth.

Later on we shall deal with this blatant contradiction; here it suffices to state that every theory, ideology, philosophy of life, was professed under the banner of truth and that the seriousness of the question whether something was true or not was always recognized and respected.

It was the doubtful privilege of Communism and Nazism to dethrone truth for the first time by showing a complete indifference toward the question of whether something was true or not, and by replacing this question with subjective measures, such as the proletarian mentality in the former and the feelings of the Nordic race in the latter. The mutiny against the spirit embodied in Nazism testifies to this excommunication of truth from all the domains of life. Conformity to the feelings of the Nordic race or of the German people replaced every objective standard of truth, goodness, beauty, and right.

In 1933 the Bavarian minister of education, Mr. Schemm, declared solemnly before the assembled professors of the University: "From this day on, you will no longer have to examine whether something is true or not, but exclusively whether or not it corresponds to the Nazi ideology."

The climax of this ousting of the role of truth as supreme judge is to be found in paragraph 24 of the first official program of the Nazi party, stating that Christianity should be accepted to the extent that it is in agreement with the feeling of the Nordic race. Even concerning the ultimate sphere upon which the eternal fate of man depends, the question of the truth of its claims has lost its importance. In the past, martyrs died in order to give witness to the truth of Christianity.

A great deal of blood was shed in wars fought in the name of religious truth. Heretics always claimed that they professed the one true religion. Atheists of former times took very seriously the question of the truth of God's existence, and they all agreed that truth alone had to determine man's religious creed. All their arguments against God's existence had the function of defending truth. Whatever their real motives, they accepted the necessity of appealing to truth as to the ultimate judge and the undisputed presupposition for any discussion. To make the question of whether one should accept or reject a religion depend upon the conformity to the feeling of the Nordic race—that is, upon a completely contingent and subjective standard—is a species of relativism unheard-of in all human history.

The same applies to Bolshevism or Communism. Every proposition uttered by Soviet propaganda has the character of a pure slogan, of a propaganda weapon; the meaning of words has been replaced with the emotional effect they are to create in the mind of the public. For instance, when Molotov speaks of the "eastern type of democracy," it is obvious that what he means is the very opposite of democracy; or when the Soviets manifest indignation over the lack of liberty in Franco's Spain, they ignore the fact that compared to their lack of freedom it is a *quantité négligeable*.

The most drastic symptom of the dethronement of truth, however, is the way that contradictory opinions are accepted in submission to the command of the Politbureau. Before 1938, Nazi Germany was characterized as an arrogant and criminal aggressor; from 1939 to 1941 the state was pictured as unjustly attacked by the vicious plutocratic nations. The fact that a state changes its attitude toward another is certainly not surprising: it is rather a very ordinary occurrence in politics. But it is a very unusual and surprising fact that no effort is made to explain how one judgment about a system and an ideology is replaced by an opposite judgment. That this transition takes place without any attempt to justify it reveals complete indifference toward the question of truth and the cynical dethronement of truth. Truth has definitely been replaced with expediency.

In arrogating to itself the role of Providence, the state deals with truth as if it were but the result of a positive, authoritative decision. That it does so without any pretension to divine capacities makes the dethronement of truth still more obvious. The question of truth is "devalued" to such an extent that no explanation seems needed for the defense of the validity of contradictory statements. The fact that they are uttered by the state is enough.

Indifference toward the question of the truth of a thing is obviously one of the worst symptoms of the perversion and desubstantialization of the human mind. It is, of course, impossible to eliminate truth completely. In raising the question whether a thing is in agreement with the proletarian mentality, one implies that the answer to this question must be either true or false. Nevertheless, the danger of attempting to replace truth with other measures, and the disrespect for the ultimate dignity of truth, cannot be denounced strongly enough.

The role of truth in human life is so predominant and decisive, the interest in the question of whether a thing is true or not is so indispensable in all the domains of human life, ranging from the most humble everyday affairs to the highest spiritual spheres, that the dethronement of truth entails the decomposition of man's very life. Disrespect for truth, when not merely a theoretical thesis, but a lived attitude, patently destroys all morality, even all reasonability and all community life. All objective norms are dissolved by this attitude of indifference toward truth; so also is the possibility of resolving any discussion or controversy objectively; peace among individuals or nations and all trust in other persons are impossible as well. The very basis of a really human life is subverted. There exists an intimate link between the dethronement of truth and terrorism. As soon as man no longer refers to truth as the ultimate judge in all spheres of life, brutal force necessarily replaces right, oppression and mechanical, suggestive influence supersedes conviction, fear supplants trust. Indeed, to dethrone truth means to sever the human person from the very basis of his spiritual existence; it is the most radical, practical atheism and thus it is deeply linked with the depersonalization of man, the anti-personalism that is the characteristic feature of Communism and of all the different types of totalitarianism. An abyss separates this decomposition of human life and of the human person from the attitude expressed in the words of St. Augustine: "O

Truth, Truth, how inwardly did the very marrow of my soul pant for You . . ." [1]

ꝺꝺꝺꝺꝺꝺꝺꝺꝺꝺꝺꝺ

Although the dethronement of truth manifests itself in the most drastic and radical way in Nazism and Bolshevism, unfortunately many symptoms of this spiritual disease are also to be found in democratic countries.

In discussions we sometimes hear the following argument: "Why should your opinion be more valid than mine? We are equal and have the same rights. It is undemocratic to pretend that your opinion is preferable." This attitude is extremely significant because it reveals the complete absence of the notion of truth, the tacit elimination of truth as the norm for the value of an opinion.

In ignoring the fact that the very essence of every opinion involves a thesis that affirms or denies some fact, such people deal with opinions as if they were mere attitudes of a subject, such as a subjective mood. The immanent theme of every opinion is truth; the only thing that matters here is whether or not it is in conformity with reality. The question of who proffers an opinion, on the contrary, has as such no importance whatever for its validity. We must realize that this argument should not be interpreted as if it meant: Your opinion has no greater chance than mine to hit upon the truth. Such an argument would not ignore truth

[1] *The Confessions of Saint Augustine,* trans. F. J. Sheed (New York, 1942), III, 6, p. 47.

or tacitly eliminate it. It would, on the contrary, presuppose the existence of objective truth if only by denying that our adversary has a greater capacity for finding truth. Patently, this argument could have meaning only if our opponent, in proffering an opinion, claimed its acceptance because *he* proffered it; or, in other words, because his authority should guarantee the truth of his opinion. Without raising here the question whether or not such a claim can be justified, there is no doubt that the equality of the intellectual capacity to grasp truth cannot be correctly inferred from the ontological equality of men or from the equality of their rights as men.

Yet, this argument is generally not meant as a refutation of an opponent's pretension to a greater competence to find truth, but as a plea for the equal value or validity of both opinions. Thus it simply ignores the fact that the validity or value of an opinion depends exclusively upon its conformity to reality; that is, it no longer questions whether a statement is true or false. This argument deals with an opinion as if its value depended exclusively on the person uttering it. Therefore, this modern type of man does not examine the arguments of the adversary; he is not interested in the correctness of his conclusions, the evidence of his premises, but in completely turning away from the fact that the opinion confirms or denies, he only proclaims: "My opinion is as good as yours because we are all equal." Whereas in the totalitarian systems the true function of a proposition—namely, that of stating truth—has been replaced by the merely instrumental character of being a weapon destined to create a certain effect in the mind and soul of the public, a means of propaganda, in the democratic countries there is a trend to regard an opinion as merely an expression of the mind of an individual. In both cases the essential function of any proposition and opinion that purport to conform with being is ignored and eliminated.

The argument, "My opinion is as good as yours," does not imply the tacit presupposition, "We are both unable to find truth, or at least we cannot know whether we are able to do so, and thus both our opinions are wrong or doubtful." It rather implies that both opinions are equally good, valid, though contrarily opposed to each other. And this brings us to another slogan disclosing the dethronement of truth. It is the often-repeated "It is true for me, but it may not be true for you." The truth of a proposition is essentially objective; a truth which as such would be valid for one person only is a *contradictio in adjecto*. A proposition is true or false, but it can never be true for one person and false for another. The statement that a certain action is morally good may be true or false; but if it is true, it can never be false for any other person. The suffix "for," implying a relation to an individual, is essentially excluded in truth.

Even if the content of a proposition refers to an individual only, it is incorrect to say that it is only "true for him." If Paul says, "I arrived Friday in Pennsylvania Station in New York," the truth of the proposition implies no relation to a single person, and if it is true, it is true for everyone. The fact that only Paul arrived Friday in Penn Station and not Harry, in no way reduces the truth of Paul's arrival to something valid only for him. The arrival applies only to Paul and not to Harry, but the fact that Paul arrived is a reality, and thus the truth of the statement "Paul arrived" is in no way relative to him. If a man claimed that "oranges are unhealthful" because he is allergic to them, his thesis would be false and not "true for him." On the contrary, "Oranges are unhealthful for me" would be a true statement: not only true for him, but true in itself.

Summarizing, we can say: A proposition, an opinion, a thesis, can never be true for one person; if it is in conformity with reality, it is true as such, and excludes any "for."

When dealing with a relation to a person, the "for" has to be in the content of the proposition, as a part of the affirmed reality, such as, for instance, "Oranges are unhealthful for Paul," or "This work is too much for Peter." If, on the contrary, someone omitted to mention the relation to himself, or to any other person, in the context of the affirmed state of facts, and said "Oranges are unhealthful" only because he is allergic to them, his statement would be definitely false and in no way truc "for him."

Certainly a person can say: "It seems *to me* to be true." But in saying so he in no way refers to a truth that is valid only for him. In saying, "It seems *to me* to be true," he wants either to state that according to *his* conviction it is true, or that its truth is not yet ascertained. When the stress is placed on the "seems" and not on the "to me," a restriction is imposed on our affirmation. Instead of saying that it is so, we say that it only seems to be so. The "seems" necessarily implies a relation to someone, that is, to the mind of a person. But obviously the restriction of my knowledge or conviction concerning the truth of a proposition which the "seems to me" expresses does not imply its being "true for me." The fact that it is not absolutely certain whether something is true or not affects in no way the character of truth as such. If it is true, it is not only true for me but true in itself. Nevertheless, for the moment I am only able to say, "It seems to me to be true," which is equivalent to "It is probably true."

If the stress is placed on the "to me," if, for instance, someone opposed the opinion of another by saying, "To me, this does not seem to be true," the notion of truth in its integrity is equally presupposed. This statement is equivalent to the proposition "*I* believe that this is true." Of course the subject is necessarily involved, as soon as the question of considering a thing true or false is at stake. It is always a person who considers a thing to be true or false; the truth attributed to a statement by one person but not by another, however, is never a truth for someone. The relativity implied in the statement, "It seems to be true to me," is in reality nothing but the expression of the fact that I hold something true or false. Certainly *I* hold it true or false, but by the truth or falseness that I ascribe to a thing I mean a truth or falseness in itself. If a proposition does not correspond to reality it is false, independently of whether or not it is held by one person or by many. We can thus clearly see that the statement, "It seems to be true to me," differs essentially from the statement, "This is true for me." The first is a correct expression of a conviction concerning the truth of a proposition; the second is a nonsensical *contradictio in adjectu.* The first in no way dethrones or desubstantializes truth; the second is a typical symptom of impairment of the notion of truth, a complete indifference toward the question of whether a thing is true or not.

Thus the slogan, "This is true for me" reveals a radical disinterest in the question of truth, a complete misunderstanding of the nature of truth, a dethronement of truth as the judge of any thesis, opinion, or theory.

There are still other symptoms of the dethronement of truth. Sometimes it would seem that for many persons the notion of progress assumes a function somewhat analogous to that of the Nordic race in Nazism and of the proletarian mentality in Communism.

For these people, the two alternatives, progressive and reactionary, have replaced the alternatives good and evil. Interest in the progressiveness of a thing has absorbed the interest in the question of its truth. The meaning of the term "progressive" is nearly as vague, void, and accidental as the meaning of the "feeling of the Nordic race," or of "the proletarian mentality."

The fact that something corresponds to the mentality of our epoch is no more decisive for its truth or value than the fact that it corresponds to the mentality of former times. The concept of progress certainly *does* sometimes imply the notion of improvement, as when we speak of moral progress or progress in knowledge, progress in recovering health, and so on. But we also speak of the progress of an illness, of a decomposition, or of an enmity. Progress as such signifies only a more developed stage of an evolution, an intensification, without indicating whether it is a good or an evil that is developing.

To make of progressiveness the source of a consciousness of superiority, and the ultimate measure for the acceptance or rejection of a thing, is thus a further symptom of the dethronement of truth. Making a fetish of swimming with the stream of the present epoch, of keeping up to date, is bound up with a subjectivism that replaces the conformity of a theory, a thesis, or a proposition to reality, by a conformity to the "spirit" of a certain epoch. The "objectivity" a theory possesses because it comes to the person from without as an interpersonal reality, instead of being only his opinion or originating in his mind, is confused with the true objectivity resulting from conformity with being.

The historical reality possessed by ideas "in the air" replaces the authentic metaphysical reality of a thing, as well as the objective validity and truth of these ideas. The intoxication experienced in swimming with the stream of a certain epoch, in being supported by public opinion, in sharing in a new, unheard-of evolution, has replaced the sober and noble interest in truth, the respect for truth as the ultimate judge of every theory, every opinion and thesis.

Finally, a characteristic symptom of the dethronement of truth is the reasoning with which vicious ideologies and vapid theories are often refuted. Instead of proving the falsehood of materialism, racism, collectivism, certain people will often offer the following argument as being the most conclusive: "These ideologies are not in conformity with the tradition of our country." In the Swiss press you may find: "Nazism and Communism are not in conformity with the Swiss tradition. In France, "It is against the genius of France"; in the United States, "It is incompatible with the American way of life." Is it not alarming that even when we face these visions of hell, these false ideologies, we can trace the dethronement of truth in the very mouth of the defenders of the dignity of the person and of freedom? A deep intellectual insecurity betrays itself here: a feeling of being more sheltered and standing on firmer ground when appealing to such a completely contingent factor as a national "way of life," than when appealing to truth and objective values.

Certainly, it is not their incompatibility with a national tradition that makes these systems of government and their philosophy detestable to many people who argue this way. Their horror may be a sound response to the objective disvalue of these systems and to the falsehood of their philosophy. What is so appalling is the fact that as soon as they want to utter the most decisive and stringent argument, the most "objective" one, they have recourse to an appeal which, as such, in no way proves the value or disvalue of a political system, or the truth or falsehood of its philosophy. The dethronement of truth here assumes less the character of disrespect for truth, of a radical ignoring of the question of truth, than the character of distrust toward the question of truth, of an elimination of this question. Any recourse to truth is treated as ineffectual. On one hand, because of a basic intellectual insecurity men no longer dare to appeal to truth; on the other, they believe that the use of a completely subjective measure is a more powerful and conclusive, a sounder weapon against these errors.

If these arguments were uttered with respect to things having the character of a mere expression of national individuality, such as certain customs or cultural habits, they could be correct and certainly would in no way be alarming. Concerning, for instance, differences between forms of government, such as between monarchy and republic (which according to the doctrine of the Holy Church are equally good), such an argument would be absolutely correct. Monarchy, corresponding as it does to the tradition and way of life of England, is the right form of government for the English people; whereas monarchy would not agree with the traditions and way of life of Switzerland or the United States, and would thus be out of place there. But as soon as differences that imply either moral questions or ideologies are at stake, such reasoning clearly manifests the dethronement of truth.

In the face of these alarming symptoms, the question arises: What are the factors that have led to this spiritual disease? What are its causes?

The most obvious causes of the dethronement of truth are various forms of relativism, ranging from moderate subjectivism down to outright skepticism, which, with increasing rhythm, have become the "official" philosophy taught and professed in secular universities. Today it seems as if there were but one point in which the various non-Catholic philosophical theories agree: that is the denial of the possibility of attaining objective truth. Certainly an abyss still lies between this theoretical denial of objective truth and the really accomplished and lived indifference toward it. As it happens, in his direct contact with being, man is protected for a certain length of time from accepting the assorted absurdities he may profess in his theoretical analyses.

In general, we may observe that the voice of being is so convincing that in the lived, immediate contact with it man forgets the different misconstructions he creates in reflecting theoretically upon it. Fortunately, man is not so consistent that his direct approach to being is immediately affected by his theories. Convincing and evident data, and not his absurd theories, remain the basis of his responses. When, for example, Nietzsche saw an icy road one winter, he wept out of compassion for the poor children who might fall on it, notwithstanding the fact that in his theoretical statement he declared compassion to be nothing but a symptom of deplorable weakness and of a decadence of vitality. Yet he did not experience his immediate response as a deplorable weakness, but as something objectively justified. In their struggle against capitalism, the Marxists appealed to justice and to the rights of men, although theoretically they professed a materialism which left a place neither for ethical, absolute values nor for the rights of men. For, patently, a being which is not a person but merely a higher, more developed kind of matter can have no rights whatsoever.

Moreover, in life the direct approach to being remains for a certain period protected from the perversions of the intellectual sphere. We see, for instance, that from the Renaissance until the beginning of the nineteenth century art and culture were still rooted in the Christian heritage, notwithstanding the progressive spiritual secularization in the theoretical sphere which took place during this epoch. But this "protection," which was due to a fortunate inconsistency, does not last indefinitely. Whenever man becomes lost in errors God gives him a certain period of respite. While consuming the paternal heritage the prodigal son could live on it for a certain time. But after a little while the heritage is exhausted. Analogously, after a certain time errors in the theoretical sphere begin to affect man's immediate approach to being and will corrode and pervert his spontaneous attitudes.

This is what actually happens with respect to truth.

The century-old propagation of relativism and subjectivism, although inconsistently implying a tacit respect for truth, affected finally the direct approach to being, and created the attitude of indifference and disrespect for truth in life itself. In the long run, man does not remain inconsistent: what is professed in theory necessarily becomes at a certain moment an informing factor of man's lived attitude. Thus the responsibility of all subjectivists and relativists for the dethronement of truth must be fully acknowledged, although, due to their inconsistency, they appealed to truth in practice.

It is not, however, exclusively thematic relativism—i.e., the attack on objective truth—that is at the basis of the dethronement of truth. In Kant's gigantic system we find a complete reversal of the process and nature of knowledge. According to Kant, knowledge is no longer understood as a grasping of a being such as it is objectively—a spiritual possession of it, or an intentional participation in being, but a process of constructing the object of our knowledge. Indeed, in this deformation of the notion of knowledge—a deformation equivalent to a denial of the very nature of knowledge—Kant is as inconsistent as any skeptic or relativist is bound to be. While claiming that in reality knowledge consists in the construction of an object, he clearly does not say that he offers us a construction of knowledge, but that he has discovered the real, authentic nature of knowledge. His knowledge of the nature of knowledge is introduced as knowledge in the classical sense of that term. Clearly, Kant is doomed to inconsistency, as is any skeptic, because in trying to deny such ultimate data as being, truth, or knowledge, he necessarily presupposes them in the same breath.

Yet, having banished the knowledge of any objective, metaphysical reality, Kant introduced the dangerous notion of the *postulate* and thereby replaced truth with indispensability. Certain fundamental metaphysical facts now became no longer accepted because of their truth, i.e., their reality, but merely because of their indispensability for ethics. The shift in the direction of the postulate, or of the substitution of an indispensable presupposition for truth, manifested itself already in the *Kritik der Reinen Vernunft*. The great aim of Kant's construction was to save mathematics and science from Hume's skepticism, or, as it can be said, to prove the possibility of synthetic judgments *a priori* in mathematics and in the sciences. Thus his entire way of proceeding has somehow an apologetic character. Instead of the pure thirst for truth and the genuine "wondering" of Plato and Aristotle, instead of the undistorted exploration of being as such, the most fundamental metaphysical and epistemological facts are approached under the viewpoint of a defense of such a relatively contingent and secondary object as science. Whereas Plato discovered in *Meno* the existence of an absolute objective truth independent of experience in the sense of observation and induction,[2] Kant was concerned with the hypothesis destined to save the possibility of synthetic judgments *a priori,* and he ended by sacrificing the notion of objective truth on the altar of science. He

[2] Cf. D. von Hildebrand, *Vom Sinn Philosophischen Fragens und Erkennens* (Bonn, 1950).

sacrificed objective truth for the sake of *a priori* judgment. Great and profound as the transcendental deduction is as a method, as an analysis of concrete experience by delving always deeper into all its metaphysical presuppositions, it is a typical case of the surgeon who declares that an operation was carried out very successfully—but unfortunately the patient died. Obviously if we abandon both the notion of knowledge as a grasping of being such as it is objectively and the notion of truth that is not merely relative to the human mind the possibility of synthetic judgments *a priori* no longer matters.

Freedom of the will, the immortality of the soul, and even the existence of God were no longer to be proved as real facts and professed as truths, but were now merely assumed because one could not do without them. The substitution of practical indispensability for truth is a perversion of the greatest consequence. The most important facts upon which everything else depends are no longer approached from the point of view of truth, but merely from the point of view of their indispensability for ethics. Here the question of truth is even expressly suspended. Here we encounter a complete reversal of the true hierarchy of being. What is true is no longer the basis of our attitudes because it is true, but we accept a fact arbitrarily as if it were true, because we need it as basis for our moral life.

Some important distinctions must be made here. The notion of the *postulate* must not be mistaken for necessary presuppositions which we are entitled to infer from certain real data. It is in the name of objective truth that we infer, e.g., the existence of a *causa prima,* from the existence of contingent beings. The existence of a contingent being guarantees our knowledge of the existence of an absolute being. This conclusion is absolutely correct. It is rooted in genuine interest in reality and is based on a valid, classical procedure leading to the attainment of knowledge.

The postulate, on the contrary, does not claim to be accessible by the process of inferring a cause from its effects. Rather, it must be presumed in order to safeguard a thing which for practical reasons (in the broader sense of the term) we cannot afford to sacrifice. The postulate shows the same lofty suspension in the air as does the categorical imperative; just as important and fundamental as is Kant's insight into the categorical character of moral obligation, as unsatisfactory is his ignoring of the value from which this categorical imperative issues. He deprives the categorical imperative of its ontological basis and even sees in this privation the condition of its objective validity. There is no *reason* that would guarantee the existence of a postulate. It involves, on the contrary, the elimination of the question of truth and the replacement of truth by practical indispensability. Without asking whether or not something is so in reality, we have to accept it for the sake of its indispensable role in our life.

The postulate must also be distinguished from the hypothesis. The hypothesis, though a construction offered as a possible explanation of a phenomenon and not the necessary result of an inference, is nevertheless an attempt in the direction of finding a truth, and with the demonstration of its plausibility it is definitely placed under the aegis of truth. It appeals to our "critical" reason and not to our "practical" reason.

Third, we must distinguish between the indispensability of the postulate and the classical character of a truth manifesting itself through its fundamental congeniality with the totality of the cosmos. We mentioned above that man in his direct contact with being often contradicts his own theories. But we are not thinking of the fact that in our weakness we often do not act in conformity with the principles our reason accepts as true. We mean that in confronting being in an immediate, lived contact, reality gives the lie to many absurd theories which are the result of abstract constructions and are obtained by deducing them by means of doubtful syllogisms, from vague premises, instead of by listening to reality. Someone, for example, may theoretically deny the existence of objective moral good and evil, but as soon as he is confronted with a noble moral action or a mean, wicked attitude, forgetting his artificial theory, he will grasp the elementary reality of objective moral values.

This correction of abstract, artificial theories by the undistorted voice of reality, the voice of reality which has not been silenced by prejudices, takes place in the frame of knowledge and appeals to truth instead of to practical indispensability. Thus we are not merely *postulating* the objective reality of moral values when, in arguing against the moral relativist, we proffer as argument the fact that he admits objective moral values in his life—at least in his response of indignation or admiration. We are by no means suspending the question of truth by arguing so. We do not rely on the mere statement: "You have to give up your theory because it does not work. You must, in any case, suppose objective moral values, or you will not get far." No, we claim, on the contrary, that in the naïve and immediate contact with being the relativist grasps intuitively the reality of the very thing he tries to deny on the theoretical plane. We claim that his theory is not the result of a real insight, but of the artificial combination of prejudices, unproved, tacit presuppositions, sophistical pseudo-arguments; and that it is even dictated by many motives that are extraneous to the sphere of reason, being an intrusion of pride and concupiscence. Conversely, the conviction informing his immediate contact with being is the result of a real perception; it is the result of the convincing power of reality, which reveals itself independently of all prejudices, and though the knowledge in question is not a critical and systematic one, it gives evidence of the objective existence of moral values, and is genuine and valid knowledge.

Various ways exist in which a metaphysical reality may reveal itself to our mind, and it would be ridiculous to claim that only the way that can be deduced *more geometrico* addresses itself to our intellect. The sphere of our intelligence reaches farther than that of mathematical deduction. To appeal to an experience of a thing immediately given[3] without being able to prove it with arguments does not mean to suspend the question of truth and to substitute something else for it. The question of truth surpasses by far the range even of that which can be grasped by human intelligence. We shall see, later on, that a false, fossilized rationalism has its share of responsibility in the dethronement of truth, although in a more indirect way. But the postulate definitely involves the suspension of the question of truth and its displacement by practical indispensability. By taking refuge in the notion of the postulate, we accept a metaphysical truth not because it manifests itself in its intrinsic truth and classical character, but we only behave "as if" it were so, because we "cannot manage without it."

The line that leads from the postulate to Vaihinger's "as-if philosophy" and to pragmatism is obvious. And it is not difficult to see that the attitude that manifests itself in these theories has, in gaining more and more currency, contributed largely to the dethronement of truth.

A third cause of this dethronement is historicism. The relativism that results from seeing every philosophy and theory as a mere historical phenomenon tacitly eliminates truth as the norm and fixes our attention on the significance of an idea as an expression of a certain

[3] Cf. D. von Hildebrand, *Christian Ethics* (New York, 1953), pp. 1–19.

epoch. This attitude is brilliantly described by C. S. Lewis:

> The Historical Point of View, put briefly, means that when a learned man is presented with any statement in an ancient author, the one question he never asks is whether it is true. He asks who influenced the ancient writer, and how far the statement is consistent with what he said in other books, and what phase in the writer's development, or in the general history of thought, it illustrates, and how it affected later writers, and how often it has been misunderstood (specially by the learned man's own colleagues) and what the general course of criticism on it has been for the last ten years, and what is the "present state of the question." To regard the ancient writer as a possible source of knowledge—to anticipate that what he said could possibly modify your thoughts or your behaviour—this would be rejected as unutterably simpleminded.[4]

The poison of historicism is specifically dangerous for two reasons. First, historicism is a perversion of valuable and important truths. Second, it is not directly concerned with the denial of objective truth, but in focusing itself exclusively on the historical aspect it tacitly eliminates the question of truth. In stating that historicism is a perversion or an abuse of valuable insights we are thinking of the undoubtedly true fact that in the exploration of philosophical truths there exists a historical rhythm; for the full philosophical *prise de conscience* of fundamental facts requires a certain historical moment—its hour in history, requires, moreover, that an evolution of ideas has prepared this possibility,

[4] *The Screwtape Letters* (New York, 1944), pp. 139–40.

and so on. It is not by accident that Aristotle's discovery of the four causes was preceded by the pre-Socratics, by Socrates, and by Plato. Hegel's theory of a development of the objective logos in history has undoubtedly hit upon something true, questionable though his entire conception may be. But interesting and important as the historical aspect of a philosophical theory may be, it is secondary in comparison with the question whether the insight is true or not, whether the theory is in conformity with being or not, and to what extent it is so.

Historicism does not content itself with examining the role of the rhythm of history in the exploration of truth, nor with the limitations due to certain historical intellectual situations, but it reduces the entire significance of a religious, metaphysical, or ethical conception to its historical function. When we, for instance, hear praise of St. Augustine, or of St. Anselm, we expect to find some concordance between the position of the author and one of these saints; but we expect it in vain. Enthusiastic and apparently sympathetic as the appreciation of these philosophers may be, any position toward the truth or falsehood of their ideas is avoided. We find it stated only how great they were for their time, how well they expressed their time. Intelligence and spiritual *stature* have become here the decisive norm, and no longer the truth or falsehood of their insights.

Skepticism and positivism, which deny objective truth, are comparatively more concerned with truth. Rebellion and enmity against objective truth at least regard the question of truth more seriously than does historicism. Historicism treats the question whether a theory is true or not as of no interest, or even as if it were a naïve and crude approach to an opinion, a philosophical system, or an ideology.

Its approach to religion is specifically typical of historicism. Whereas atheists still take seriously the question of God's existence, the historicist seems not even to understand the immanent pretension of religion, but looks at it merely as an interesting cultural and historical phenomenon. He treats the different religions with equal sympathy and expounds their doctrines with apparent respect and benevolent understanding. He views them apparently not "from without," but from within, but this "from within" means an immanentism that has once and for all tacitly eliminated the great decisive question whether this religion is true or not. In reality this seemingly sympathetic approach is the ultimate climax of a distorted view from without, because it deprives religion of its innermost meaning, which is truth, divinely revealed absolute truth, which the *Credo* affirms and for which martyrs have shed their blood. In cutting off faith from truth—its objective correlate—and in making of it an interesting expression of the human mind, historicism desubstantializes religion to a greater extent than the man who denied God in the name of objective truth.

A typical fruit of historicism is the position toward the Holy Church taken in the *Action Française,* and especially in the writings of Charles Maurras. Maurras praises the Church for its cultural and political function, the value that it embodies in history, and above all for its "latinity." He eulogizes the Church because it is so wonderfully pagan. Is this favorable judgment of the Church not a greater offense and misunderstanding than a furious attack on the part of Protestants, who reproach her for being not faithful enough to Christ? Unthinking and shocking as it is, the Protestant reproach takes more seriously than did Charles Maurras the claim of the Church to teach divine truth and the words of Christ.

Finally, the predominance of a psychological approach and the triumphant march of psychoanalysis also had their share in preparing the dethronement of truth. The interest in psychological reasons—why a person utters an opinion, affirms a thesis, holds a position toward a theory—has replaced more and more the interest in the question of the truth of this opinion, this thesis or theory. Justified as this approach may be in many cases, indispensable as it is to examine this question in order to judge a person and decide how to deal with him, as soon as it supplants the question of the truth of the opinion, a disastrous perversion takes place.

When upon hearing a theory concerning metaphysical problems one asks only what psychological motives may be behind it, instead of examining whether or not this theory is in conformity with reality, his approach is in many respects perverted: he should be primarily interested in the *truth* of this theory. A sound approach is primarily concerned with the content of a thesis, with its claim to being true. There must be some special reason to justify turning away from the object and focusing on the soul of the person who utters a theory. One reason can be that we are professional psychologists. But even in this case, the question whether an opinion is false or true has an eminent importance for our psychological analysis. If the theory is true, special psychological motives are not necessarily required in order to explain why a person professes this theory. On the contrary, man's normal motivation for holding an opinion is the compelling force of the reality his intellect grasps. It would certainly be bad psychology to eliminate *ab ovo* the possibility that a person's motivation for holding a thesis is simply the fact that reality has disclosed to him that it is so. As long as a theory is true, or insofar as it is true, there is normally no other motivation at stake than the truth, and all that we have to analyze in the mind of the person holding the theory is the nature of his knowledge, conviction, and judgment. This analysis, however, concerns only the explanation of how a person can acquire knowledge and objectivate it in a thesis; but the reason for holding an opinion remains the truth of this theory or the existence of this fact. In errors we may look for "psychological" reasons, but as long as a true statement is in question, we have no reason to look for subjective motives.

Thus we have to state that even a psychologist must inquire whether a theory, a statement, or a judgment is true or not before he can examine the psychological condition of the one uttering it, because the question of its truth has a paramount importance even for deciding whether a psychological problem is involved or not.

Of course, there can also be extraordinary cases in which we have to look for psychological reasons, though the judgment or the thesis is true. A person may be either hysterical or cut off by his self-centeredness from all genuine contact with being and the world surrounding him. In this case, even if he states the truth, we do not believe that his statement is the genuine result of the dictates of being; though the content of his judgment is true, we doubt that a real interest in truth is at the basis of his judgment. On the other hand, he may be dishonest, and then we mistrust him to such an extent that *what* he is saying no longer matters, but exclusively *why* he is saying it. We presume in such a case that this man's statement is merely a means for attaining a practical purpose. This psychological approach is the only reasonable one when we have to deal with persons who have completely dethroned truth, such as, for example, Hitler or Stalin. But the fact that when dealing with an opinion or a statement, in case of moral perversion or mental abnormality, the only thing to do is to turn to a psychological research, clearly reveals that such an approach is inadequate under normal conditions. The factors which are responsible for an illness and which explain its origins cannot be present in the healthy person. If the statement is false, it may be necessary to examine whether psychological reasons answer for the error, but as mentioned above, we must first ascertain whether it is true or false. Moreover, the psychological explanation of the error does not dispense us from a rational refutation of it. In order to help the person who, for moral reasons, cleaves to a wrong theory or even merely acts as though he did, we, for our part, must start from the firm ground of objective truth. Only if we ourselves start from the basis of that which is objectively true shall we be able to help other persons to overcome the moral and psychological obstacles barring them from truth.

Above all, we must realize that the real nature and validity of the higher acts of the person can be understood only by including their object in our analysis. It is the very nature of conviction to be convinced *that* something is so; of the nature of joy, to be joyful *about* something. As long as we ignore the object to which the conviction or joy is responding, its nature and its value, an evaluation of the act is impossible.

It is a basic error to regard personal acts as though they could be understood independently of their intentional character; a basic error to approach this ambient as though it were composed of mere states and accessible to an immanent and causal analysis, undermining the interest in the truth of an opinion or judgment and substituting for the question, "What is he stating?" the question, "Why is he stating it?"

Here one may rightly ask: If relativism, pragmatism, historicism, psychologism have brought about the dethronement of truth, what is the cause of all these different "isms" and, especially, of the fact that they did not remain in the theoretical realm, but infected and corroded the naïve, lived approach to being?

The present educational system has its responsibility in the corrosion of the masses' naïve approach to being. In our epoch, and especially in the United States, the ideal that everybody should be instructed, that everybody should have an intellectual education, is widespread. The conviction that everything can be learned if properly taught, that a high good would be unjustly withheld from a person if he did not receive his share of the modern treasure of knowledge, is at the basis of this ideal. Without discussing the truth of these two presuppositions, we can easily see that the new situation concerning the instruction of the masses opens the door for spreading pseudo philosophies among the public. Through the new educational ideal, the decoction of all these destructive "isms" is poured into the minds of young people and respectfully accepted by them. To this, let us still add the perpetual "massage" of our minds by movies, newspapers, magazines, and radio, and we can understand why the dethronement of truth today remains no longer the province of certain professors, but has successfully infected the immediate approach to being of the average man.[5]

Nevertheless, it is true that we must dig still deeper in order to reach the ultimate roots of the dethronement of truth. Indeed, we do not claim that we are able to unveil the origin of a perversion of the mind such as this, because ultimately it is as mysterious as the origin of evil itself. But the one element behind those theo-

[5] Cf. "The New Tower of Babel," pp. 14 ff.

retical denials or eliminations of truth, as well as behind the entire attitude manifesting itself in these theories, is accessible to our analysis. It is the apostasy from God, the rebellion of man against the Father of all truth, the refusal to accept the condition of a creature and the glorious vocation of being an image of God. In trying to shake off the *religio*—i.e., the fundamental dependence upon God, the obligation toward God in which we are embedded, the ordination toward God—we necessarily become victims of falsehood and corrode our basic relation to truth. The attitude of *non serviam,* the desire to follow the temptation of *eritis sicut Dii,* the rebellion against God, is the ultimate root of the dethronement of truth.

The problem of showing how to overcome the dethronement of truth is by far more difficult than that of tracing its sources. We shall restrict ourselves in our analysis to inquiring how we should fight against it.

First, the classic refutation of all brands of skepticism and relativism should time and again be emphasized. As far as the influence of relativism and positivism is concerned, we have to eradicate it with philosophical arguments. We should not fear to appear old-fashioned, antiquated, or even banal in repeating what loses neither its power nor its profundity by having often been stated. The fact that the modern denial of objective truth has more the character of an unchallengeable presupposition than that of a positive thesis—as in skepticism—must not divert our attention and lead us to a suspension of this question while we deal with philosophy. It is a kind of snobbishness which hinders many thinkers from restating again and again the strict refutation of all forms of skepticism. They shun the appearance of being unindifferentiated, primitive, and without any sense for the problems of our epoch. Certainly the unmasking of the intrinsic contradiction and inconsistency of any and every denial of objective truth should not be proffered as a merely schematic and bloodless formula. To repeat it again and again does not mean to repeat a stereotyped formula; on the contrary, its every repetition contains a full insight which, in all its inexhaustible power, unmasks the empty and nonsensical character of every radical skepticism. As Goethe rightly said: "Error finds ceaseless repetition in deed, for which reason one must never tire of repeating the truth in words." [6] We must realize that the inconsistency of radical relativism is such that a philosopher who even tacitly presupposes the denial of objective truth has objectively condemned his entire philosophy. Even more, every scientist who denies the possibility of attaining objective truth utters senseless words, mere babbling.

We must insist on the ridiculous inconsistency of all those who profess a denial of objective truth and simultaneously arrogate objective truth to their theory. Noth-

[6] "Maxims and Reflections," 331 (1826), *Goethe, Wisdom and Experience,* selected by Ludwig Curtius, trans. H. J. Weigand (New York, 1949), p. 126.

ing can be more fatal to a theory than to deny in its content what it necessarily presupposes in the very act of affirming. We must not cease unmasking the inevitable, flagrant contradiction that is necessarily involved in every attempt to deny objective truth and the possibility of its knowledge. More and more contradictions are heaped upon this immanent contradiction between the content of an affirmation and the implicit formal claim of every affirmation as such. When offering argument or even writing whole books to prove the thesis that absolute truth does not exist, these relativists presuppose various facts as incontrovertible: first, the premises from which they start arguing; second, the validity of the principles of logic on which their conclusions are based. As soon as they suspend the validity of either one of the above-mentioned presuppositions, their arguments or their theses lose all power and collapse completely.

Likewise, we must stress again and again that Kant's dissolution of the authentic meaning of knowledge as the grasping of a being such as it is objectively (or, to use the traditional term, as the intentional partaking of the very nature of a being) by replacing it with the notion of the construction of the object, implies an immanent contradiction. Thereby Kant claims to grasp the nature of knowledge such as it is, and to offer not merely a subjective construction of what knowledge is. The fact that he considers his thesis as a fundamental discovery, as a "Copernican turning," clearly testifies to this claim. Thus we encounter here an immanent contradiction in the interpretation of knowledge, analogical to the one which is part and parcel of any relativism with respect to objective truth. In *claiming* to reveal to us the real nature of knowledge, Kant presupposes the notion of knowledge which he denies in the content of his thesis.

Again, analogically, this contradiction is clearly to be found in pragmatism. When pragmatism claims that truth means nothing but usefulness and that a proposition is true when it is a useful basis for our practical tasks, truth in its authentic meaning is implicitly presupposed. The pragmatist wants to prove that truth is really nothing else than usefulness and claims that this statement at least is true and not only useful. If he were to deny this, the meaning of his thesis would collapse completely. Likewise, he refers to truth in its authentic sense in all his premises and conclusions. In proffering arguments for his thesis, the pragmatist tacitly presupposes his premises to correspond to real facts, and presupposes in his conclusions the truth of logical principles. Even the statement that a concrete idea is useful presupposes truth; it involves the claim that the idea is truly useful. All attempts to deny objective truth and to change its meaning or the meaning of knowledge necessarily involve an immanent contradiction, because truth and knowledge are elementary, ultimate, evident data, presupposed in any affirmation and thesis. He who tries to deny these ultimate data behaves like a man who wants to jump behind himself.

If we want to fight the dethronement of truth, we must above all abandon a predominantly defensive attitude in the philosophical arena. For centuries the philosophical energy of many Scholastic philosophers has been absorbed by a distorted defense of Thomism. The question whether some philosophical theses proffered by a non-Catholic or by a Catholic philosopher is true or not seems to have become equivalent to the question whether it can be found directly or indirectly in Thomism.

Instead of trying to understand a thesis from within and to confront it with reality, frequently one has only approached it in remaining imprisoned in a certain traditional set of concepts and often even in a traditional vocabulary; without taking the trouble of consulting reality by an immediate approach to it, one has only confronted the thesis with a Thomistic textbook, and condemned it as soon as it stated anything which had not been said in it.

An unfortunate, implicit misconception of philosophy is here at stake. Philosophy is often identified with a logically consistent system in which everything must be fitted with everything else. Though Descartes' ideal is blamed as rationalistic, an equally rationalistic notion of philosophy and process of philosophical discovery is unconsciously presupposed. It is a "logicization" of reality and its mysteries. Chevalier opposed this kind of rationalism when he said

> We have had to wait until these past years, we have had to wait until this very war (1914) for Pascal the thinker to be given his true rank: the first. It is be-

> cause the war has reminded us or has revealed to us what philosophy should truly be: not a vain dialectical game of concepts, but the answer to questions that man asks himself when facing death.[7]

Whether a Thomist or not, a true philosopher struggles to delve always deeper into the inexhaustible plenitude of being, to discover new aspects and truths; and in doing this he will be more faithful to reality than to a "system" which he has built up. We notice in the history of philosophy that great philosophers did not shrink from asserting what reality discloses to them, even though it may not fit into some theories they have built up. They do not let themselves be severed from reality by concepts they have formed and theses they have reached as deductions from former insights.

Sometimes the philosophical Eros—the "wondering" and the desire to consult reality time and again—are replaced by a preoccupation with defending every detail of the Aristotelian-Thomistic system. What is legitimate and even obligatory with respect to revealed truth as formulated in the dogmas of the Church is here unconsciously applied to a philosophical system.

This attitude not only frustrates any philosophical exploration but also does injustice to the great philosophical achievement of St. Thomas. Instead of understanding that it is impossible to remain faithful to the conception of a great philosopher if we do not strive to discover for ourselves the data from which he took his point of departure, the intuition that was the starting point for his concepts, it is often believed that it suffices

[7] *Pascal* (Paris, 1925), p. 7.

to give abstract definitions of concepts and it seems satisfactory if the path leading from one concept to another is smooth and logically correct.

Sometimes these philosophers have nothing in common with the one whose disciples they claim to be beyond mere terminology. Thus, also from the point of view of doing justice to a great and venerable philosopher, we must go back to being, to an intellectual intuition of the reality he discovered, and we must be more anxious to remain faithful to this discovery than to his conceptualization of it, and all the more, than to his terminology.

But above all we must be more eager to find truth than to examine whether something is in agreement with the system of a philosopher, great as the philosopher may be. If a genuine appreciation of a philosopher by a *historian* of philosophy already requires that the philosopher's thought be confronted with reality and measured by truth, we must in a *systematic* exploration of reality give way *a fortiori* to the imperturbable inquiry after truth.

This true appreciation implies that we never let ourselves be barred from the immediate approach to reality by becoming prisoners of fossilized concepts, by being unable to leave a smooth, habitual track, frustrating any fertile contact with being and any enrichment, completion, and correction of the philosophical achievement of a great and venerated master. In this sense, Sciacca writes in honor of Blondel's memory:

> This magazine . . . will continue to honor his memory and to participate in his thought in the only way in

> which one truly honors the memory of a philosopher and in which one demonstrates the vitality of his speculation: in deepening the problems of Christian philosophy with Blondel, but beyond Blondel.[8]

Some philosophers seem to confine true philosophical work to a mere elaboration of all immanent consequences of the Thomist system, a work that can be achieved by intellectual acuteness without consulting reality. Others see the main task of philosophy to lie in an integration of modern scientific and psychological results within the system—that is to say, its enlargement by elements belonging to the extra-philosophical sphere. It is clear, however, that every true philosophical work consists in an always renewed and continued exploration of being and in the confrontation of all the concepts of the school with reality. Only this can give us the possibility of appreciating fully the discovery that led to the formation of these concepts, and of enriching and completing former results, of proceeding to new differentiations, and sometimes of eliminating artificial problems resulting only from too vague a use of certain terms.

If we gratefully accept Aristotle's distinction of the four causes and the metaphysical relations based on them, should we therefore *ab ovo* exclude the possibility that there may be still other metaphysical principles than those discovered by Aristotle? Why should we not have the right to explore being with the same

[8] "Maurice Blondel," *Giornale de Metafisica,* Luglio-Agosto, 1949, p. 330.

unprejudiced approach and openness of intellect as did Aristotle?

> Let the foregoing suffice as our account of the views concerning the soul which have been handed on by our predecessors; let us now dismiss them and make as it were a completely fresh start, endeavoring to give a precise answer to the question, "What is soul?" [9]

Why should it be excluded *ab ovo* that an unprejudiced analysis of being could in an analogous way surpass Aristotle's conquest of the four causes, as his discovery surpassed the knowledge of the pre-Socratics? Do we in any way do injustice to Aristotle's discovery, do we deny the truth of his distinction between the *causa efficiens* and the *causa finalis,* if our analysis of reality compels us to admit that there exist still other causes or fundamental metaphysical relations? Is it not the worst offense to a great philosopher for us to presume that he claims to have discovered everything, seen all problems and answered them completely—which pretension would be precisely the absolute antithesis of the Socratic statement: "I know but one thing, that I know not"? [10] What, precisely, distinguishes the true philosopher from the mere schoolmaster is the consciousness that the plenitude and depth of being surpass incomparably the range of true insights he may have gained.

True philosophy must always clearly distinguish be-

[9] *De anima* II, *Basic Works of Aristotle,* trans. Richard McKeon (New York, 1941), p. 554.

[10] Plato *Apology,* 20 ff.

tween truths that are the result of real insight, referring to data given or accessible through strict deduction, and mere hypotheses which can never be verified or proved themselves, but can only be judged according to their plausibility.

The distinction between empirical knowledge and the absolutely certain knowledge of strictly necessary, intelligible facts in Plato's *Meno* is, for instance, a classical example of a fundamental philosophical discovery, of an insight based on something evidently given. The anamnesis theory, on the contrary, is a typical hypothesis destined to explain the possibility of *a priori* knowledge, but proffering propositions and theses which cannot be verified as such, because they refer to what is accessible neither to our experience (intuitive or inductive) nor to deduction.

The distinction between a proposition referring to a sphere of reality accessible to intellectual intuition or to deduction and a proposition referring to a sphere of reality inaccessible to intuition and deduction, neither denies the necessity and value of a hypothesis nor excludes the possibility that a hypothesis may be objectively in full conformity with reality. But as soon as we no longer distinguish them clearly, and deal with a hypothesis as if it were an undeniable, evident fact, we risk barring ourselves from reality. We then approach being through a network of concepts resulting from a hypothesis; and not only do we interpret every datum in the light of this hypothesis, but we lose contact with the immediately given. We then infer how being should be from concepts that are stripped of their original content; above all, we waste our intellectual energy on artificial problems arising exclusively from the fossilization of certain concepts. Being has so many mysteries which are philosophically yet unexplored; it offers so many data of which the philosophical *prise de conscience* is still lacking, that it seems unbelievable that so much intelligence should be squandered in solving imaginary problems arising only from nonexistent alternatives, or from the extension of certain concepts into spheres of being in which they have no *fundamentum in re.*

Many terms are used in so broad a manner that the differences in meaning (which are precisely what matters) are not really grasped. Will, for instance, is used as embracing all meaningful affective responses—i.e., love, admiration, esteem. What today we have in mind, however, in speaking of will is the specific response directed to something not yet real, the content of which could be circumscribed as "thou shalt be," an act which is free in the full sense of the word and which is the master of all actions. The will in this specific sense is the *causa exemplaris* for every attitude we include in this term. And thus in calling love an act of will, we falsify *de facto* the very nature of love, the specific quiddity of love, which distinguishes it from all other responses. We must realize the danger resulting from using certain terms when we define them in a completely analogous sense but use them in a much more univocal sense as soon as we apply them *in concreto.* Such is the use of the term *finis.* If we want to use it in a sense in which it covers every meaningful direction toward something, we must not only clearly distinguish this general term from the original meaning of *causa finalis,* but also we must not allow the "means-and-end" relation to remain in our mind as the hidden pattern of finality.

We must come back to a lively continuation of the magnificent process of real philosophical exploration leading from the pre-Socratics to Socrates, Plato, Aristotle, St. Augustine, St. Bonaventure, St. Thomas Aquinas, to a full restoration of the "wondering" before the cosmos in its inexhaustible depth.[11]

Only a philosophy which is filled with the true philosophical eros, which reveals to us in all its rhythm the words of St. Augustine: *Quod desiderat anima fortius quam veritatem,*[12] can do away with the discredit of reason and truth and restore full respect for truth in all domains of life. Only a philosophy that is deeply rooted in a live awareness of the plenitude of being will restore to philosophy its organic role of opening our eyes to the mysteries of being, of deepening our lived contact with being, and preparing our spirit for the infinitely superior truth of revelation, the true sense of *philosophia ancilla theologiae.* To the inconsistency of modern subjectivists who strive for ideals the ontological presupposition of which they deny—like the upright atheist of 1848 who thanked God every morning that He made him an atheist—there must be opposed a full consistency, that is, a lived truth, revealing in our approach to whatever practical problem that we are "rooted and

[11] Cf. D. von Hildebrand, *Christian Ethics,* pp. 1–19.

[12] *Tract. 26 in Joannem,* 4, 5.

founded" (Eph. 3:17) in the fundamental natural truths, and above all, in Christ, "who is the solution of all problems." How often do we meet Catholics who deny Christ and even fundamental natural truths as soon as they face social or political problems in the practical realm of life! To allow the light of natural and supernatural truth to penetrate fully every problem is the principal way to restore the full respect for truth as the supreme judge in all questions and as the norm of our attitudes.

The task of the re-instauration of truth implies, above all, the eradication of the moral roots that led to this disastrous attitude toward truth. In "Catholicism and Unprejudiced Knowledge" [13] we shall deal with this aspect. Here it may suffice to stress that, in order to re-establish the respect for truth and the acceptance of its character of supreme judge, any merely intellectual counteraction will not suffice. If abuses of distorted reason have led to the dethronement of truth and opened the way for the deification of all that is inferior to man and to human reason, only the suprarational light of Christ can re-establish truth in its God-given place and bring reason back to its ordainment toward truth; in other words, re-establish even reason and save it from self-destruction.

[13] Pp. 132 ff.

THE NEW FUNCTIONALISM
IN THE
LIGHT OF CHRIST

WRONG ALTERNATIVES play a fundamental and disastrous role in the history of the human mind. Errors are often fought by means of an antithesis that implies a worse error than the one it claims to overcome. A striking example of this to be seen in our epoch is the idol of neutrality. Claiming to be the champion of true objectivity, it has never ceased to attack cheap emotionalism or ungenuine pathos. Its creed, typically embodied in the "new functionalism" that arose after World War I, has set up a prosaic norm of objectivity as the antithesis to all forms of emotion. It has opposed every romantic gratification of one's own feelings, every evidence of pathos, all forms of ungenuineness which give false, high-sounding names to things, and all examples of overembellishment and insincerity. In architecture, a new style under the aegis of the "new functionalism" has developed in reaction to the ungenuine, overornate architecture of the years 1870 to 1880. This period was one of *mauvais goût* and tawdriness, a period in which railway stations were adorned with Greek capitals in cast iron, in which city halls and post offices were decorated with tin towers supposedly resembling Gothic strongholds. It was the time when one found in every home a closed "company parlor" crammed with unnecessary and tasteless ornaments of the "gingerbread" variety, rooms overcrowded with furniture and paintings of every description.

The style of the new functionalism, on the contrary, shrinks from any kind of ornamentation; its aim is to build buildings "objectively." Everything should be pervaded by an exclusive finality. Anything not immediately related to this end should not be tolerated (LeCorbusier). Buildings should breathe a prosaic, mathematical, mechanical atmosphere. In the name of the new functionalism one wages war, for example, in music, against every type of "feeling." Above all, pathos, ecstasy, ardor, solemnity such as may be found in the works of Wagner and Beethoven are called deviations. Music should be music and music only, and, consequently, prosaic and without a soul.

We may prescind here from the value of the artistic creation of this new functionalism, as well as from its thematic program. Rather, we are interested in the ethos of this new functionalism that we actually find in the most varied realms of life, and in the question: To what extent is this ethos compatible with a Christian conception of the world?

We are here concerned with the attitude toward the world which lies at the very roots of this new functionalism—an attitude not confined solely to partisans of this ideal. This ethos of cool neutrality, of prosaic distance, which calls every enthusiasm "exalted" and every ardor ungenuine, will accept dynamism and strength, but will reject the specific affective intensity of emotion[1] and of love. This ethos is closely linked with an overemphasis on the immanent law found in

[1] Emotion is used here in the sense of "being touched" (Rührung) [Translator's note].

the different realms of life. It is often encountered now. It is displayed in the attitude of the sexes toward each other, in neutral comradeship, in the predominant role played by a sportive attitude, in the professional as well as in the religious life, and in man's relation to nature. In examining this ethos, we must, above all, ask ourselves: Is it truly what it pretends to be? Is it truly objective? Does it truly deserve the honorable title of "objective" which it arrogates to itself? Moreover, is it really the antithesis of sentimentality, ungenuineness, intrinsic falseness, tawdriness, gaudiness? We heartily approve of any condemnation of these negative qualities. We are all in favor of a rejection of the architecture of the 'Eighties. But is the ethos of the "new objectivity" truly a positive antipode of this spirit, or is it not rather an effort to expel Satan with the help of Beelzebub?

The very fact that in music works of such noble depth and grandeur as those of Wagner, and even those of the unique genius of Beethoven, are labeled as unobjective and empty pathos, as ungenuine and emotionally weighted, and are therefore rejected, should make us suspicious and should lead us to ask the following question: Is this new objectivity not opposed to ardor and intensity as such?

What is the meaning of objective? We call an attitude objective when it is determined by those elements which are, in a given case, the thematic and decisive ones.

A judgment on a work of art is objective when it is measured by artistic standards. It is unobjective if one rejects the fine work of a rival with an unfavorable opinion because of personal advantage. It is equally unobjective if one approves of a work merely because the critic is a friend of the artist in question. Any prejudice against a thing is unobjective because one's affirmation or rejection is not motivated by elements thematically pertinent to this realm, but by points of view alien to the theme in question. This unobjective bias can be, at one time, motivated by unthematic, rational consideration, and, at another moment, conditioned by emotional attitudes. There is a cool, calculating unobjectivity and one that is passionately blind. This distinction as such is irrelevant to the question of unobjectivity.

An impression can be unobjective when the image of a thing or of a person is distorted by prejudice; i.e., the impression is necessarily false because of a biased position one has previously taken.

An attitude, too, can be as unobjective as a judgment. The decisive point always is whether a person acts according to the objective *logos* of a thing, or whether he acts arbitrarily; whether a person's impressions, attitudes, and judgments are adapted to and adequate to the object in question, or whether they are formed and determined by unthematic elements.

We can refer to objectivity both in a narrower and in a broader sense of the term. In the broader sense, every inadequate judgment or attitude is unobjective, i.e., every false judgment as opposed to a true one, every inadequate enthusiasm, love, admiration, as opposed to adequate responses—responses proportionate to the value of the object. In this sense we can call objective only true judgments, correct impressions, and adequate responses to an object. Every error, every deception is unobjective, whatever its object might be.

When, however, we consider the word objective in the strict sense of the term—the meaning that is most frequent—the truth of a judgment and the adequacy of our attitude are not necessary. From this angle, no point of view should be admitted which is unrelated to the theme under consideration. In this sense, a wrong judgment on a work of art will be unobjective only when based on extra-artistic points of view, such as economic and political considerations, or on sympathy or antipathy for the artist. In other words, the narrow meaning of objective has one requirement only; namely, that we are exclusively governed by the point of view pertinent to the realm in question. If, due to a lack of understanding, a wrong judgment or an inadequate attitude ensues, we should rather call it incorrect than unobjective. An incorrect artistic judgment resulting from a lack of taste or from a moral error in judgment or attitude—such as enthusiasm for an idol of false honor—is objectively inadequate, but not unobjective in the strict sense of the term.

How can we define the ethos that we term objective? Is there one specific ethos that we can designate as "the ethos of objectivity"? Is it perhaps the kind of ethos which we find incorporated in this new functionalism? Is the ethos of the new functionalism—an ethos of prosaic neutrality, of cool distance, free from every kind of enthusiasm and ardor, an ethos which is anti-affective, in which every fullness of the heart is immediately interpreted as exaggerated and exalted—is this ethos required by objectivity in our sense of the term? Are the two connected in any way at all? The idea that an ethos of cool distance, critical reserve, and prosaic neutrality is specifically objective has not been confined exclusively to the "new functionalists." And yet, is it not evident that the ethos objectively required, the ethos that is adequate to the content and inner meaning of a respective field, must vary according to the different realms in question? It therefore seems impossible to call a specifically slanted ethos the objective one, independently of the nature of the particular field under consideration.

Is one acting objectively if, when contemplating a sublime spectacle, such as a glorious sunset, one is in no way moved by it, but remains in an attitude of prosaic neutrality and in a state of critical reserve? Does one act objectively if, when witnessing the sufferings of others, one remains cool and indifferent? He rather is objective whose heart is wounded by these sorrows. Can we call that person objective who, in his relationship with other men, never goes beyond an attitude of flat neutrality, a person for whom the richness of a mind, the goodness of a heart, the loveliness and charm of a personality never awaken love and enthusiasm? Is a man unobjective because he sheds tears when reading the Gospels? Is a man unobjective because he is immersed in loving adoration of God? In the religious sphere, would we call that man objective who dispatched his religious duties in an attitude of prosaic neutrality, and who went to the Communion rail maintaining a cool distance, in order to accomplish this "duty" effectively? In other words, the question of which ethos is objective cannot be solved in itself. All in all, it depends upon the nature of the object at stake, and, in the last analysis, upon the true nature of the universe. If the true meaning of objectivity consists in the fact that the attitude of the subject is formed by the objective logos, by the spirit and nature of the object one is confronting, then the answer to the question, which ethos is objective and which one is unobjective, must take its point of departure from a consideration of the structure of the cosmos as a whole, and of the single realms of being within that whole.

Is the world truly so soulless that an ethos of cool distance and prosaic neutrality is the objective, adequate, basic ethos? What conception of the world forms the basis of this new functionalism? How does this ethos stand when measured against the Catholic conception of the world?

The ethos of the new functionalism is often considered to be objective because of several assumptions that are really basic errors lying at the very roots of its conception of the world. The existence of values in their specific nature is overlooked as a whole, and the cosmos is considered to be a mere tissue of neutral ends. When we want to make a machine, its construction is dominated by the specific aim toward which we strive, apart from mechanical requirements. The finalism of the construction as such is unrelated to the question of whether the aim has a positive value or a negative one, or is neutral altogether. This finalism is typically manifested in the formal relationship existing between an activity and its end. The question of the nature of this aim, i.e., whether it is valuable or not, is not yet touched upon. As long as we consider the world only as being a tissue of neutral finality, the question of value is completely left aside. If we contrast the world of values, the world of goodness and beauty, to ends in this formal, functional way, we turn to something entirely new. When we say that a melody is beautiful, that an action is good, or a thought deep, we do not in any way mean that these things are the end of something else, but that they are important in themselves, that they are drawn out of neutrality and indifference because of their mysterious fullness of content. We mean to say that they reflect God, the Sum of all values, in a special and direct way, and that they praise and glorify Him as such, because of their value. It is impossible to try to reduce this unique essence of values to a formal finality, for these values possess a mysterious content, full of import. They stand before us in their sovereign majesty, and demand that we respond, independently of our subjective wishes and strivings.[2] The value character, on the contrary, justifies the functioning of something as an end. That which has a value should be an end, but a thing is not valuable because it functions as an end. In the last analysis, a thing is only meaningful as an end if it is itself valuable or in some way serves a value, and not vice versa.[3]

As soon as this difference between value and end is clearly grasped, one immediately sees what a tremendous difference lies between an end which has a value in itself—as, for example, the moral development of a man—and one which is, as such, neutral—as, for example, money, which is only related to a valuable end through the act of its being used. Furthermore, one discovers that within the frame of ends having a value there is an enormous hierarchy with regard to the rank of their values. Consequently, one realizes that in establishing an end as meaningful and necessary, and even as valuable, nothing is said as yet concerning the rank of its value. This fact leads one to observe that the indispensability of a thing should not be confused with the rank of its value. Eating is more indispensable than culture. It is not, however, more valuable thereby.

The first basic mistake underlying the conception of the world held by the new functionalism consists in the fact that it reduces a cosmos rich in values to a grayish network of neutral aims. A second mistake,

[2] Cf. D. von Hildebrand, *Christian Ethics,* chaps. 3 and 18.
[3] *Ibid.,* chap. 8.

closely linked to the first, is a misunderstanding of the spiritual and meaningful character of the person's affective responses to value. Because one disregards the nature of values, one also fails to realize that they call for an affective response on the part of the person. One fails to grasp that the adequate response to a sublime work of art is emotion[4] and enthusiasm, and not a mere acknowledgment of its value. One overlooks the fact that a heroic moral attitude of our neighbor, an act of love toward his enemies, calls for veneration and enthusiasm on our part and not just for a cool, appreciative confirmation. Here again we meet another deep-rooted misunderstanding. The point of departure is the consequence of a wrong alternative: on the one hand, one places the realm of spiritual, meaningful acts, which are, without more ado, identified with intellectual attitudes; on the other hand, the irrational realm of vague emotional states, the unspiritual and biological sphere to which everything affective as such is relegated. One ignores the fact that the affective realm does not only consist of emotional states; that, in an analogy with the intellectual attitudes, they, too, are attitudes meaningfully directed toward an object, and that attitudes such as love, admiration, enthusiasm, and longing are just as spiritual as are theoretical attitudes. Love is not a meaningless state causally produced by the intermediary of some other thing, as is the case with depression, fatigue, or a mere state of unrest; love is a meaningful response directed toward an object, a response that is rich pre-

[4] Cf. note, p. 104.

cisely in affective content. This is also true in the cases of veneration, enthusiasm, and longing.

It is evident that the spiritual character of these attitudes differs from that of theoretical ones. But this fact does not make them inferior. These attitudes are not less luminous, spiritual, and meaningful on that account. It is true that in contradistinction to intellectual attitudes affective responses relate to the vital sphere, and that when they reach a certain intensity they involve also the corporeal sphere; for instance, experiences such as crying from emotion[5] and all other accompanying organ sensations that follow affective attitudes. They are, however, but accompanying manifestations of these attitudes and do not constitute the attitudes themselves. They in no way change the specifically spiritual character of these attitudes as such. Are we entitled to call something unspiritual because it touches the person to such a depth that it also affects other spheres? The meaningful, rational nature of these spiritual, affective attitudes does not consist in disowning their affective character and evincing the distance and coolness of intellectual probing. Rather, their spiritual, rational nature consists in the fact that they address themselves meaningfully to an object in a specifically affective manner, with full ardor. It further consists in the fact that they are consciously and meaningfully related to an object, and that this connection is no mere link of efficient causality. Moreover, their spiritual character manifests itself in the fact that they

[5] Cf. note, p. 104.

can be freely sanctioned by the person.[6] Thus, the fallacious supposition that every affective attitude is as such unobjective is due to a twofold error: first, a failure to grasp the world of values; second, a disregard for the intentional direction and spiritual, meaningful character of affective responses. As a result, these responses are confused with mere emotional states.

Actually, values call for affective responses on our part and we respond adequately only when we respond affectively. The specific character of responses due to values, and consequently of objectively adequate responses, is precisely an affective attitude, such as love, enthusiasm, or veneration. Moreover, the adequate response to the Sum of all values, the Absolute, is nothing short of loving adoration.

If the world were nothing but a network of neutral ends, then surely love, veneration, enthusiasm—indeed every emotion and every solemn attitude—would truly be unobjective, because they would not be called for by the nature of objects, precisely because the objects motivating these meaningful attitudes would not exist. In such a case, an ethos of cool distance and prosaic neutrality would be the only objective one. But because the world is not a network of neutral ends, but a cosmos full of resplendent values, because it reflects and heralds in a multitude of ways the Sum of goodness and beauty which is God, the attitude of the new functionalism as a basic attitude of mankind is unobjective. Therefore, it adorns itself quite illegitimately with the noble title of objectivity.

[6] Cf. *Christian Ethics,* chap. 25.

True, there are certain realms that partially call for this attitude of cool neutrality and distance; for example, the sphere of business accounts, mere matters of fact, the testing of a machine for its use, and, to a certain extent, the domain of scientific knowledge. But even in this last case it is partly true only, for here also a certain Eros is presupposed in order that the world of being may reveal itself in all its fullness and depth to the knowing eye.

But there are still other fundamental errors concerning the structure of the cosmos which account for the identification of this neutral ethos with objectivity.

First of all, we refer to an erroneous concept of objectivity. Objective and impersonal are used as equivalent terms. Because the human person alone can, as a result of his free will, set himself in contradiction to the objective logos of things, the sphere of the human mind, as such, is considered to be an antithesis to objectivity. The concept subjective, in the pejorative sense of unobjective, has meaning in the realm of human-personal beings only, whether it be within the psychic life itself, or among the objectivations of the human mind, such as in the spheres of art, science, and the whole of culture, and can never be applied to the world of nature, neither to organic nor to inorganic things. For this reason the personal sphere as such is regarded as unobjective. A distrust of the personal as such arises from a lazy resignation toward the many "unobjective" attitudes of men and their egocentric tendencies. One turns to the ever-genuine and "objective" character of impersonal beings, and yet it is precisely the personal sphere that can spiritually harmonize with that which is objectively meaningful, and which can possess a depth of objectivity never reached by impersonal nature. For objectivity ultimately means conformity to God's thoughts, i.e., an adequate reflection of God. Impersonal nature can hardly escape reflecting God, but this reflection of Him, the Person *par excellence,* can never be so adequate as the one a person can accomplish.

The adequate response of a person and a morally right attitude on his part are, though personal and free, much more objective than anything impersonal can ever be, because they reflect God more adequately and specifically. This cult of the impersonal, so often met with today, also ignores the fact that the personal being, a luminous, awakened, and conscious being, is not an oscillating or shifting thing, but is being in a fuller and more substantial way, compared to which impersonal being is only being in a weaker, analogous sense.

This erroneous concept of objectivity has gained currency far beyond the circle of partisans of the new functionalism, and makes its appearance in more or less disguised forms. It is even to be discovered in the religious ideal of many Catholics. The compass of this error which, in the last analysis, fails to consider the personal character of God, cannot be overstressed. From a psychological point of view, we might compare this flight into the impersonal, a flight conditioned by our love of objectivity and antipathy for subjectivity, to an attitude which, because of its horror of sin, would idolize the sphere of animals and material substances because obviously they cannot sin.

Another error closely linked to this one is also characteristic of the new functionalism, and can be labeled as a typical heresy of our time. We refer to the exaggerated importance granted to impersonal goods as compared with personal values.[7] The misunderstanding of the nature of personal beings leads one to consider the importance of a man to consist primarily in the production of impersonal goods, and in his accomplishments for the state, the nation, art, science, or the sphere of economics. Achievement, as such, is placed above personality. Efficiency ranks above virtue and holiness. And within the range of impersonal goods the preference is given to those that are least stamped by personal imprint, because these goods are considered to represent the truly "serious" part of life, such as the sphere of economics, technique, civilization, politics, and national power. Pure knowledge and art, or, above all, communities such as family and marriage, are relegated to the background. This is so true that among impersonal goods the preference is given to those in which a formal consideration of finality can more readily be

[7] Cf. "Efficiency and Holiness," pp. 205 ff.

applied, and this is done in spite of the fact that they are not ends in themselves, but possess only an objective significance in serving another sphere having a value in itself. One makes of man a mere "working machine."

Work, as such, is immensely overrated; amusement and pleasure are the only antitheses one opposes to work.[8] The hyperactivity of our epoch—the terrible rhythm of work which enslaves the person and prevents him from fulfilling the life for which he is truly called, namely, the contemplation and loving adoration of God as well as love of neighbor—clearly bears witness to this mentality. One forgets that the spiritual person does not only embody a higher type of being, but also bears immeasurably higher values than any impersonal being can ever possess. One ignores the fact that God, the Sum of all values, can be so much more adequately reflected and glorified through the person. One forgets that virtue and, above all, holiness rank incomparably higher than efficiency. One loses sight of the fact that the primary vocation of man does not consist in the production of impersonal goods, but in holiness, in the imitation of Christ, in the unhampered development of the holy life which has been implanted in him in Baptism, and this means nothing short of holy love.

Granted that for those who consider the spiritual, personal conscious being as "less objective" than the merely vital or merely material one, and primarily see in the person a servant of impersonal, terrestrial goods, the ethos of the new functionalism appears to them as objective and adequate. For here, neutrality and imper-

[8] Cf. "Efficiency and Holiness," pp. 220 ff.

sonality, coolness and the absence of any affective note are considered as synonymous with objectivity.

Finally, let us turn to one particular error: namely, the overemphasis placed upon the immanent law of things. Nowadays one refers much to the immanent law of things. In doing so, however, one confuses two different concepts. At one time one may have in mind the fact that every realm has certain laws that are proper to it: for example, the technical domain, or the domain of economics, of the material world, of music. Another time one understands by immanent law that a domain having its own value is at stake, a domain which in its perfection praises and glorifies God as such, and not only through its connection with another realm. In this second sense art, science, and community are domains having their proper value, because through their value they immediately glorify God, apart from their role for man's sanctification. Because these spheres possess a value of their own, we should be governed by their own distinctive meaning when taking a position toward them. Economics and politics, on the other hand, certainly have an immanent law in the first sense, but they do not possess values of their own. The most extraordinary prosperity has, in itself, no value. It acquires a value only insofar as, on the one hand, the sphere of economics concerns the elementary necessities of life for certain individuals, and, on the other, insofar as it serves the realization of cultural goods. Their immanent perfection as such grants them no proper value.

Of course, a truly objective point of view requires that our attitude toward every single realm of goods take its specific character into consideration—that is to say, we follow the immanent laws of economics when dealing with a problem of economics; the laws of technique when concerned with a technical problem, and so forth. Nevertheless, we should always keep in mind when dealing with these realms having a subservient character that we should never be exclusively guided by their immanent laws. On the contrary, a consideration of the values to which these realms are subordinated and which they serve should also play its role. Above all, the ethos of man should never be formed according to these elements of the immanent law of things. After all, man is a whole, and his nature resists being divided into functions—i.e., as if he were at one moment exclusively an "eating being," at another a "working being," and yet at another nothing but a "bathing being"—even though these different activities call for a certain immanent law. Even though a man's present consciousness may be more or less filled by the immanent law of these subordinate realms, yet in a deeper stratum of his being he must remain occupied with other things that are more central. In the final analysis, he must remain centered upon God. Man should always see the immanent laws of merely subservient realms in the light of their intermediate values, and, above all, keep in mind the value of the end. This vision should form his ethos when dealing with these things. Even when a realm possesses a value of its own, our ethos should not be determined by this value but must also reflect the hierarchy of values. The ultimate norm in the formation of our attitude, in our approach to every sphere and, above all, in our ethos, should always be determined by the higher value and not by the specific value of the realm in question, and in the last analysis it should be governed by the Sum of all values: God.

The exaggeration of the immanent law and especially the lack of distinction between value proper and immanent law, is paramount for the idol of the new functionalism. The question of how bathing suits should be made, for instance, under what conditions the sexes should be permitted to go swimming together, would, according to the creed of the new functionalism, be regulated by the rules proper to swimming alone. Actually, it is highly unobjective to overlook much higher and more important moral points of view, which, in their superiority, should overrule the things that are in the first instance "objective." Music that takes into account only the immanent laws of music and because of this excludes the specifically artistic meaning which is superior to it and contains its thematic value, is equally as unobjective. Architecture which deals only with the practical needs of life as being thematic, which regards a house as merely a "machine to live in" and fails to consider that a fully human life in its dimensions of depth and breadth soars far above mere hygienic considerations and the most comfortable and rational dispatching of exterior needs of life, is also unobjective. These views are unobjective because they are the consequence of a wrong conception of what the life of man is, because they illegitimately isolate single life functions, and because they make of the organic current of life a sum of unrelated, final functions of parts. In spite of all this, it is always the personal life that makes life worth living and gives it its richness of content.

How does the ethos of the new functionalism stand in relation to the Catholic ethos? This is the question to which we must now turn our attention. A glance at the Catholic conception of the world and a comparison between this ethos and the typical presuppositions forming the new functionalism immediately show us what an abyss lies between them.

1. The Catholic conception of the world is no neutral network of formal ends, but a cosmos rich in values. Because the Source of being, God, is not a neutral "All" as the pantheists would have it, but the Sum of all goodness and beauty, the Saint of Saints, it follows that beings that reflect Him will also be rich in values. Turning to the liturgy, we find innumerable places in which it is clearly expressed that the Glory of God is reflected through the created world. There is nothing more un-Catholic than utilitarianism, and there is no greater antithesis to this utilitarianism than the words of the *Gloria: Gratis agimus tibi propter magnam gloriam tuam.* (We give Thee thanks for Thy great glory.)

2. In the Catholic conception of the world there is no room for the wrong alternative of either spiritual and intellectual or non-spiritual and affective. In this religion of love, whose two great commandments are the love of God and the love of neighbor, on which "dependeth the whole Law and the Prophets" (Matt. 22:40), in this religion, which states that "God is love," the spiritual and meaningful nature of love is necessarily presupposed.

3. In the Catholic conception of the world there is no opposition between person and objectivity. For here, the absolute being is not an impersonal idea, not a sum of mathematical laws, but a personal God. For in such a conception the Sum of all intelligibility and being is a person, and the Logos is the Second Divine Person.

4. In the Catholic conception of the world man, with his immortal soul, is not primarily measured according to what he accomplishes in the realm of impersonal goods, but according to what he is.[9] Man glorifies God through his own person, when he develops the holy life infused in his soul through Baptism, when he becomes a saint, when Christ lives in him and he lives in Christ. This is the true glorification of God, supremely higher than that accomplished by all the impersonal goods man produces, infinitely more than all of his contributions to culture, science, art, and the sphere of rights. Never, absolutely never, can the human person be considered as a means for the accomplishment of an impersonal end, as high as it may rank, whether it be state, nation, or humanity. Could we think of a more

[9] Cf. "Efficiency and Holiness," pp. 209–10.

radical, more incredible expression than the Incarnation and the death of Christ on the cross, to prove the unique value of the immortal soul of every man, and the priority of being over production? What an incredibly negative value sin has here! And how incredible the value of holiness!

5. Finally, in the Catholic conception of the world there is no room for absolute independence and absolute immanent laws. Man should never consider anything or anyone exclusively from the point of view of its content, whatever it has to offer, but in its intrinsic relation to God and His kingdom.

As radically as the Catholic conception of the world differs from the one of the new functionalism, then as radically must we, Catholics, reject this ethos-without-soul as our attitude toward life. Can there possibly be a greater antithesis to the ethos of the new functionalism than the one of the saints? Think for a moment of the spirit emanating from the *Confessions* of St. Augustine, its holy emotion and ardor! Hear again the last words of *The City of God: Ecce ibi vacabimus et videbimus; videbimus et amabimus; amabimus et laudabimus; quod erit in fine sine fine.* (There we shall rest and see, see and love, love and praise. This is what shall be in the end without end.) [10]

Reflect on the life of St. Francis, his song of the sun, or on the life and writings of St. Catherine of Siena! Consider the spirit pervading the liturgy of our holy Church, this holy rest united with the deepest emotion, this transfigured peace, so filled with inner ardor, this

[10] XXII, 30.

holy continuity separated by an abyss from neutral prose and soullessness. And finally let us be filled with the spirit of the Gospel itself, for did not our Lord Jesus Christ say: "I am come to cast fire on the earth . . ." (Luke 12:49)?

Even though the new functionalism may be credited with opposing many errors, its positive content is incompatible with a Catholic ethos. There is only one true antithesis to all errors, the spirit of Him who said: "I am the way, and the truth, and the life" (John 14:6).

Translated from the German by Alice M. Jourdain.

CATHOLICISM

AND

UNPREJUDICED KNOWLEDGE

THE NATURE and conception of a university depend essentially and in the first place on the nature of true science and knowledge. It is therefore necessary to consider the fundamental problems that are the implicit presupposition of every university by its very nature—namely, those concerning the nature of true knowledge—if we are to discuss the justification and value of a Catholic university and therewith to form a critical estimate of the present-day "liberal" university.

The university of the present time rests on a fundamental principle: that all apprehension and knowledge is an autonomous function of the human mind which is and must be independent of man's will, his moral constitution, his general philosophical, not to speak of his religious, attitude, if the knowledge is to lay claim to being adequate and objective. Two points require to be distinguished here: (a) the assertion that knowledge as such is independent of the general attitude of man—that is, that in its very structure it does not involve any other attitude of the person; and (b) that true knowledge must not, as far as its content is concerned, operate with any presuppositions other than those that can be justified before the tribunal of knowledge itself.

This second point, which has often been expressly formulated, is what is meant by expressions such as "freedom from bias or prejudice," "absence of presuppositions." The first point is usually assumed tacitly and implicitly.

Reserving the second point for the moment, I turn to a critical examination of the first.

It is one of the profoundest and most characteristic traits of a spiritual personality to be able to make intellectual and spiritual contact with reality by apprehending its concrete quality and existence. The peculiar nature of a spiritual person, a conscious being, finds expression precisely in this capacity, and without this capacity a personal being would be unthinkable. A person not only has a real causal relationship to surrounding things, but is also capable of coming into contact with them in this intentional manner,[1] by, as it were, grasping them intellectually from above and by taking possession of them in the act of "knowing" them.

There are many degrees within this knowledge or apprehension: from merely taking note of a thing up to an understanding grasp of its nature; from mere apperception up to an explicit theoretical penetration of its content and a systematic exploration of the extent of its being. Again, there are many kinds of apprehension according to the nature of the thing apprehended: as the seeing of color, the hearing of sounds, the perception of a value, the grasping of a complex situation; and so there are many kinds of theoretical penetration, according to the special nature of the object and according to the nature of the problem, as, for instance, causal-genetic knowledge, historical knowledge, psychological

[1] Cf. D. von Hildebrand, *Christian Ethics,* chap. 17.

knowledge, descriptive knowledge, and last, but not least, philosophical knowledge. In most cases a scientific, theoretical apprehension presupposes in addition the merely pre-scientific perception of the thing. What are the relations between apprehension or knowledge in the widest sense of that term and the general attitude of the person?

It must be expressly emphasized that all views that attempt to interpret the certitude resulting from apprehension of the existence or non-existence of a fact as an act of the will are wholly mistaken. On being apprehended, a thing is found to exist; the question of its existence or non-existence is decided by apprehension without interference on the part of the will, and the conviction, as a *theoretical* response to be kept clearly distinct from the *practical* response of the will, registers this decision on the part of the subject, or, in other words, gives the answer that the object demands. Any endeavor to represent the determination of the existence of a fact in apprehension as insufficient, or as requiring a supplementary act of the will, misses the real nature of knowledge. The determination lies within the region of apprehension itself; the object itself is decisive for the emergence of a conviction, *it* solves the question of its existence, *it* informs me, *it* proves itself, and it leaves nothing to be supplied by an act of my will, as if the final certitude were completed by the will. Yet, even though we must reject every form of voluntarism, there are nevertheless so many connections between the apprehension and the general attitude of a person that it is equally impossible to isolate knowledge in a watertight compartment and to conceive the capacity of knowing as wholly neutral in regard to this general attitude.

For, even if knowledge is autonomous, considered both in itself and in regard to what it presents, yet the capacity of knowing depends largely upon the general attitude of the person that knows. Defective general attitudes are very apt to close the intellectual eye and to darken its vision; the right attitude, on the contrary, confers sight. I merely call attention to the most elementary moral prerequisites for an adequate apprehension: such as an honest desire for truth, absence of bias, thoroughness. It is evident that superficiality, frivolity, amateurish trifling, lack of thoroughness, dishonesty, prejudice—all of them factors that are not primarily qualities of the intellect, but of the character—fundamentally damage the power to know or the result of its apprehension.

But these are only the most obvious factors belonging to the moral sphere which influence apprehension. The history of errors, especially in philosophy, like materialism, pantheism, skepticism, psychologism, idealism, positivism, relativism, radical empiricism, and the like, shows clearly that there are far deeper connections between the general attitude of man and his capacity of knowing, and that we have to begin with the fundamental forms of man's attitude in order to appreciate the full scope of the formal and material dependence of knowledge on the very nature of man.

Attitudes of Apprehension

I start with the *negative* attitudes that interfere with the capacity of apprehension.

There we find in the first place *indolence.* I do not mean here that peripheral indolence which keeps man from any intellectual labor, "laziness" so called, but I mean a much more central, I should like to say "metaphysical," indolence of the mind which influences apprehension. I mean the indolence that renders any real penetration of the object impossible and prevents any collaboration with the meaning and essence of a thing. Certain kinds of things, which lie outside the normal visual field of a person, such as the nature of person, the nature of value, of a given situation, and of essences, or the existence of certain spiritual complexes like "epochs of civilization," or social organisms, like nations, or the existence of juridical facts, like treaties, require for their apprehension a certain *élan* of the whole man, a kind of soaring power of the mind, a willingness to abandon a customary attitude and to look in a new direction, and, above all, to allow oneself to be carried along by the spirit of the object in question and to "collaborate," to "conspire" with it. But this indolence, anchored deep down in the concupiscence of man, a *laissez-aller,* a strange, dull insistence on remaining rooted to the spot one is accustomed to, closes whole stretches of reality to the intellectual vision. As long as we remain in this attitude of central indolence, no intellectual acumen, no abundance of erudition, no merely formal capacity of apprehension can open our eyes to the understanding of the deeper strata and connections of existing things, or of higher kinds of objects of knowledge. A typical instance of the result of an apprehension darkened by this attitude is materialism, which will allow only such things to exist as are presented in a quite definitive manner; namely, within the field of vision which is most easily grasped. To a similar class belongs Association Psychology insofar as it attempts to apprehend the person primarily with the principles of the material world; in the same class we must reckon, in fact, all attempts to make of lower beings the pattern (*causa exemplaris*) of higher ones, such as the system of Freud. In such cases, any advance in understanding must begin with a totally new general attitude of the man; for no effort of the understanding as such is capable *per se* of overcoming the error, as long as this metaphysical indolence persists. It is the same attitude which, in other spheres of life, we describe as that of the "materialist."

Another fundamental attitude darkening the understanding is the incapacity, rooted in *pride,* to listen, to let things themselves speak, to allow them to instruct us. What I mean here is that pedagogic pedantry in face of the world which destroys all θαυμάζειν ("wondering") which, according to Plato, is the beginning of all true knowledge. There are people who approach things in their apprehension without the respectful desire to penetrate them with real understanding, without any thirst for truth, but rather with a supercilious repletion and a Boeotian smugness that renders open-mindedness impossible. People of that kind are blind to many things even in their *pre*-scientific apprehension; *a fortiori* in their systematic knowledge; blind to all the things that constitute the height and the depth of the world. Even their *pre*-scientific picture of the world is flattened out and deformed by reduction in scale; so their scientific apprehension lacks the vision for differentiation, mystery, and the endlessness of things. However sagacious, however thorough and industrious in their research they may be, the result of their apprehension is permeated by errors. Of course, this darkening of their understanding affects different spheres of knowledge in different degrees; philosophy most fatally of all. But wherever it appears, it cannot remain without damaging consequences: think of history, psychology, medicine, law. A typical expression of knowledge disfigured by such schoolmasterly metaphysical pedantry is the explicit rationalism of the Age of Enlightenment; so is the mania for superficial systems that bear no relation to actually existing things, force everything into a few miserable categories, and hasten to reduce all sorts of things which in their particular being constitute fundamental phenomena to something known, because such minds will not admit that "there are more things in heaven and earth than are dreamt of in their philosophy."

Worse still is the attitude of definite *ressentiment* which rebels against the objectivity and autonomy of things and especially against the existence of objective values. It resents being bound by an objective validity. It prevents any real "making friends" with an object, any willingness to listen to the voice of things, and it does so, not as a conscious gesture, but—much worse—as an unconscious fundamental attitude. It blinds the eye of the intellect toward the most patent truths, not so much to their material content as to their evidence or to their inner necessity; as, for instance, that a straight line is the shortest line between two points, or that twice two is four. This attitude prevents any illumination, because at bottom it does not want to be illuminated. This is the attitude of the radical skeptic, be he called Gorgias or otherwise, or that of the relativist who repeats with deep satisfaction the absurd thesis of the relativity of all values. In face of such minds no arguments are of the slightest use, however convincing they may be: they will not admit the convincing power of argument. Nothing but the abandonment of their fundamental attitude, only a conversion, a relaxing of the orgasm of their pride, can give them sight and lead to a liberation of their intellect. All the results of their knowledge are misled and misleading as long as this cramped pride is not relaxed, however sagacious, however clever they may be, and however "scientific" their methods. We may remember the world of Nietzsche's thought, in which the source of all his error and of his blindness to the true moral values is so clearly displayed in his fundamental attitude, or the tragic figure of Max Scheler, all of whose conclusions in his last anti-Catholic period are so unambiguously inspired by his moral attitude. Perhaps it is precisely in the sphere of the apprehension of values that the blinding effect of such a false general attitude can most easily be detected, and the root of every blindness to moral values has to be sought in such an attitude.

Lastly, there is a fundamental attitude of lack of spirit, of *distrust* toward things, which disturbs the understanding and condemns it to impotence. I mean here that constitutional distrust which renders a man incapable of understanding the simplest set of facts, because he cannot muster the necessary courage to entrust himself to the object, and because it seems to him an act of rashness to reach a definite conclusion at any point whatever. Perpetually he refers the decision to a further court of appeal, and avoids a definite "Yea" or "No" even in the most patent situations. This attitude in the intellectual sphere corresponds in the moral sphere to the running away from every responsibility. I do not mean that in the intellectual sphere the final decision rests with an act of the will: this, as explained before, is not the case. The decision rests with the object; our will does not come in question. All the same we must open our minds and make contact with the object to the extent of being able to follow up this objective decision subjectively; but in the case of the metaphysical coward and doubter, it is precisely this necessary friendly contact with the thing, this having an open mind with regard to it, that is lacking. With his preconceived distrust he avoids having anything to do with the thing lest it should inform him or give him the decisive answer; he, as it were, stops up his ears to it. The expression of this attitude is to be seen in an unmistakable tragic skepticism, especially in the ceaseless demand for a criterion, in the dislike of all intuition, in mistaking the highest and most evident connections for artificially propounded axioms, in the distrust of all material understanding, in the preference for purely formal rather than material knowledge, in the tendency to regard illusion as normal (apperception as *hallucination vraie*), in the incapacity to distinguish between evident and non-evident facts, and in a false ideal of scientific accuracy and exactness.

True knowledge must be unprejudiced. In its search it must not rest upon facts that are incapable of withstanding the test of reason. Neither is true knowledge formally a function of the general attitude of man, as if the *result* of knowledge, instead of being given by the object, were rather the *object* of the apprehension itself or dependent on the will and attitude of the knower. Nevertheless, the knower must assume the *right attitude* in order to grasp the thing as it is, to let it speak for itself without interference, to allow the understanding to proceed unhindered and to work itself out in its specific function without deformation or obstacle. A false attitude, just like inherent defects of the intelligence such as stupidity, muddleheadedness, or idiocy, deforms the power of apprehension and obscures its content. The right attitude, on the contrary, clears away all obstacles from the path of a full and pure exercise of the understanding and delivers knowledge from its fetters.

Now, the right attitude is precisely the opposite of

metaphysical indolence, a certain winged alertness of the mind, peculiar to the humbly loving, reverent personality, in contrast to the merely concupiscent self. I mean here not a merely formal mobility of mind, a formal capacity for differentiation, which many possess who nevertheless lack all real contact with things, nor that intellectual agility which so easily turns knowledge into a sport and, without ever really collaborating with the objective world, turns intellectual somersaults, that formal nimbleness which the sophists possessed in so high a degree and the unphilosophical world rejects as sheer "dialectics." I mean, rather, that quite consciously directed alertness of a man which enables him to be affected by all genuine values, to surrender himself in a value response of love and will to all real goods, "to keep step" and to "conspire" with the object of his understanding. I mean the general resonance of the mind which makes man free, which produces a response to value in the moral sphere instead of eternally seeking for pleasure, and in the intellectual sphere implies following the cue given by an object, being led by it, being able to vibrate in unison with its *ratio*—the contrast to "stick-in-the-mud" laziness, the antithesis to all dullness. The right attitude is further one of reverent yet loving open-mindedness, in opposition to the schoolmasterly pedantic superciliousness. The same reverent attitude which, in the moral sphere, produces the yearning to participate in the world of values, and especially in God, yields in the intellectual sphere the thirst for truth, the desire to participate intentionally in the real world, the metaphysical open-mindedness of a man who desires to "receive," who will not prescribe to nature *its* laws, who is willing to listen to the universe and to the wealth of its mysteries. It is that attitude which St. Bonaventure means when he says at the opening of his *Itinerarium mentis in Deum:* "These things can be understood only by one who is, like Daniel, a man of desire"; a willingness to "become empty," the power to keep silent and to let things speak for themselves. It is a reverence filled with the awareness of the depth and wealth of the cosmos, which rejects all pedantic violence done to it, which approaches things with the readiness to do justice to the profundity of things —the very contrast to the familiar "chumming-up" with the universe—and an inner willingness to be subordinate and to serve.

This attitude in no way prejudges the content of understanding in particular cases. It merely liberates the understanding, creates the conditions requisite for the full development of objective apprehension, and renders it in the fullest sense unprejudiced. An understanding resting upon this attitude does not by any means "romance" enthusiastically about things; no, it alone, by reason of its open-mindedness and selflessness, is capable of understanding anything in its own peculiar essence: great things in their greatness, small things in their smallness, simple things in their simplicity, differentiated things in their complexity, a whole in its wholeness, independent parts in their autonomy, the sublime in its sublimity, sanctity in its own singular mysteriousness—because it alone allows the object to speak for itself, which is, after all, the nature and soul of all true understanding. The attitude which, so to say, makes understanding a gift to itself is, moreover, reverent in contrast to frantic pride and all resentment against things. It is a liberated inner freedom, which, not rebelling against truth, does not feel the existence of objective truth as an oppression and restriction, but as liberating and rejoicing. Again, it means the inner willingness which is not closed against even the most unpleasant truth, which is really free from bias, ready to make friends with things, open to the proof of all objective existence, not looking at things through a colored lens that allows only such things to pass into the understanding as do not offend our pride and our self-complacency.

And, finally, this attitude which permits understanding to develop without prejudice is also that of metaphysical courage and faith. It is willingness to embark upon the great venture of letting oneself be carried along by things, a simple, sane, intellectual readiness to listen to their voice. The same attitude that will not shirk moral responsibility will also meet things without the prejudice of distrust which dims the vision for evidence and for the differences between what is and what is not evident. It is an unbiased, trusting attitude which does not render man uncritical or gullible, but merely enables him to take that step, essential to understanding, which creates a real contact with things, moves with them, opens to them the intellectual eye and ear. Just as the man obsessed with scruples moves in a perpetual circle and no longer understands the clear voice of conscience, no longer perceives the difference between good and evil, between what is and what is not permitted, so does the constitutional coward and skeptic in knowledge. For there exists the type obsessed by scruples in understanding, and he, so far from being more exact, more thorough, or more critical than the trusting man, is, on the contrary, less objective, less thorough, and less critical. For all exactness and critical reserve presuppose the clear distinction between what is and what is not evident; the uncritical attitude consists precisely in *not* grasping this difference, and it is just as uncritical to deny from constitutional distrust the evidence of proof as carelessly to consider unproven truths as evident.

Deformation of the Understanding

Before dealing with the influence of religion on this liberating attitude of the individual I want to sketch briefly a few typical but constitutional deformations of the understanding, serious generic errors which, in affecting the content of knowledge, have their repercussions in darkening the vision of the mind and permeate the whole understanding and conduct—errors typical of certain classes of men and falsifying fundamentally their picture of the world.

Here we find, first of all, what I should like to call an *eidetic blindness*. The person suffering from this defect lacks the vision for the real features of things, for their *eidos,* for what is essential and significant in a thing, in distinction from all accidental and secondary features of the concrete specimen. This class is represented by men who conceive the step from the concrete thing to what is generic or typical merely as a reduction to the average, incapable as they are of grasping the immanent significance of a thing, that which it tends to embody; they mistake the permanent average for what is essential and typical. They are faced with the simple but false alternative: *either* the concrete thing with all its accidental features (further confusing incidentally the accidental features as essential with the really constitutive and essential elements)—in other words, an unintelligent statement of the material fact viewed merely from outside; *or* a generalization obtained from a statistical average, a mediocre, anaemic, and mechanical pattern. They operate with a false conception of truth and reality: they *either* take the isolated specimen in its undifferentiated accidental being, without understanding its significance and immanent ideal, to be the only existing reality, and consider the significance of a thing, the thought of God embodied in it, as a mere phantasm, or confuse it with the threadbare, bloodless, artificial, unreal, abstract pattern; *or—per contra—*they consider the average pattern as the true thing and arrive at a typically pedantic schoolmasterly violation and deformation of the wealth of all things.

We need but remember the identification in medicine of the concept of health with the "average case" or the theory of Lombroso concerning genius and insanity, which regards everything deviating from the average as abnormal without distinguishing between a more fully realized ideal exceeding the average and a falling short of the ideal. Such men mean by common sense the average form of a *pre*-scientific reflection, instead of regarding it as the classical aspect of the cosmos as found in immediate naïve experience. They are incapable of grasping either form or meaning and consider all these distinctions in history and psychology as artificial quibbles. They propose to deal with the history of art without any sense for art and without taking the value of the work of art into account. They are afraid that to go beyond a dull statement of fact or arid statistics means leaving the *terra firma* of reality. They pursue biology without grasping the nature of life, psychology without grasping the nature of the person, sociology without understanding the true essence of community. In philosophy they are without comprehension for the world of essences, for the *veritates aeternae*—i.e., necessary, intelligible truths, and cling to a dreary empiricism. They hope to apprehend reality, approaching it wholly from outside, with the help of experiment and statistical information and the collection of material data, and deride in their helpless blindness all analysis of essences as idle dreams. They consider their very blindness as a sturdy sense of reality: the lower a thing is in the order of existence the more reliable it seems to them; an instinct appears to them as more real, as more solid than an act of the mind. In ethics they try to deal with morality on the basis of the *success* of behavior without even discussing the qualitative difference of good and evil. In art they are aware only of the alternative between a dreary naturalism with its slavish copying of accidental, unessential detail, with its studio-atmosphere, its undressed persons instead of nudes—or, on the other hand, an equally dreary classicism and a mechanical, artificial, pale idealization.

In life they are incapable of penetrating to the deeper layers of things, they boast of the pseudo realism of the "practical" man, of a false common sense, incapable as they are of freeing themselves from the trivial alternative: the so-called realist vs. the so-called idealist. In the one they see a man with a sense for the realities of life, often a mere clinging to the most obvious externalities of it; in the other an idealist, that is a dreamer (or, as they prefer to call him, a mystic), blissfully unsuspecting that the mystic is precisely he who, bursting through the fetters of this whole pedantic alternative, is nearest of all to true reality, nearest to the *ens realissimum,* God. They are the Boeotians who consider the economic sphere as the real and only serious aspect of life, while they consider knowledge, art, love, as mere luxuries.

A second generic deformation of knowledge is the *false ideal of amplitude* (if I may use that expression). It is a formalistic blindness. What I mean is the confusion of amplitude with the formal range of a concept. This type fails to grasp qualitative amplitude, the amplitude the higher value possesses, because it contains *per eminentiam* the lower. A person of this class will consider an object as wide in proportion as it is more abstract, he confuses infinity with indefiniteness. He harbors, in consequence, a curious *ressentiment* against all material knowledge, because it narrows him down and oppresses him. Purely formal knowledge seems to him more distinguished, purer, freer. In ethics he confuses material ethics[2] with casuistry; formal ethics strikes him as grander, less fettered. His religion is pantheism. It seems to him to degrade God to formulate His attributes. Even His goodness, His wisdom, seem to him a limitation of His absolute amplitude and comprehensive fullness. Revelation strikes him as objectionable without distinction of its quality: the really oppressive anthropomorphic conception of God like the pagan's, as much as the Epiphany of God in the sanctity of Christ which *per eminentiam* contains everything. He hates dogma and every dogmatic religion; the mystery of the Incarnation is to him the scandal of scandals. He fails to understand the divine beauty shining in the face of Christ, this quite definite, quite concretely formulated sanctity, which represents not a synthesis of opposites, not a combination of contrary qualities, but a totally new quality of the Divine and the Holy, coming from above. He misunderstands the fact that Christ is the Alpha and Omega of the cosmos, in whom, despite all concreteness and definition, all other values are contained *per eminentiam.*

In art this type shows a similar resentment against all perfection, against all clear formulation. It seems to him flat and limited. He sees amplitude and infinity only in the endless vista of problems, in things that are unsolved and undefined. He finds depth and width only in the tension between the desire of the artist and his capacity to execute it, in fragmentary results. He fails

[2] Cf. Max Scheler, *Der Formalismus in der Ethik und die materiale Wertethik* (Halle, 1921).

to understand that true amplitude is comprised in the very quality of value, that boundless width is the more perfectly expressed the more completely and perfectly a work of art is realized, such as the dying slave of Michelangelo or the Ninth Symphony of Beethoven. In life he will shy at every limitation; he will be happy only when getting on to something new. He would like to get up in the morning as if there had been no yesterday. He lacks continuity. He confuses license with true freedom, and is insensible to the real oppressiveness and limitation of indefiniteness and chaos.

Indeed, with an increase of this blindness, the very existence of an absolute truth becomes intolerable to him, because it involves a determination and a limitation of arbitrariness and indefiniteness. He misconceives so completely the peculiar nature of truth and its power of deliverance that he detaches the absolute claim of truth from its quality as truth and treats it as if it were the claim of an error. It is a form of metaphysical libertinism, as in that terrible and notorious utterance of Lessing which places the endless search for truth above the possession of truth. In the end this type lapses into a peculiar paradox: preferring formal knowledge and at first finding a refuge in the wide-meshed net of formality, he ultimately recoils even from this clear definiteness, escapes into formlessness and chaos, and rebels against every kind of form as narrowing and arresting.

A third generic error is constituted by *neutralism* or a *constitutional formal blindness to value.* I mean the type of person who recognizes no values, only purposes or ends; for whom the world is a web of mere purposes. He fails to see that an event, dominated by a purpose, permeated by a teleological end, does not merely, for that reason, belong to the class of things significant in themselves, of values *per se.* He reverses the real relation of end and value. He insists that being an end constitutes a value, instead of understanding that, on the contrary, only being a value makes a thing legitimately and significantly into an end. For such a man, the universe is not a cosmos of values, but merely an arid organization of ends.

This type also misconceives naturally the whole range of affective life. He equates spirit with intellect and will, and puts all the significant value responses—such as love, enthusiasm, reverence—on a level with merely unintentional feeling states, as no more than meaningless sensation. He is faced with the false alternative: on the one side, spirit and intelligence; on the other, the merely organic life, the unilluminated, non-intentional sphere to which he takes affective responses also to belong. The result is a false conception of objectivity and adequacy of reaction. He misconceives the fact that, in face of a universe of values and especially in face of God, the only response that is adequate and objective—i.e., corresponding to the object—must also comprise the affective sphere. Values demand an affective response. If a person remains untouched by the suffering of another, and is moved by the beauty of a great work of art or of nature to nothing but an intellectual statement of fact, he lacks in the highest degree objectivity and adequacy of response. For all true objectivity and adequacy consist precisely in accepting the object and its *ratio* and in meeting its demands. Such a man follows a wrong conception of life, empty of affectivity and of yearning, of a drabness that in no way does justice to the true qualities of the world. He accordingly rejects all real affective ardor and God-intoxication as sentimentality or subjective bombast. He cherishes a false ideal of reality; only what subserves a temporary end seems to him real and genuine.

Here lies also the root of a false conception of science—namely, of the mistaken idea that an attitude which keeps things at a distance and does not allow itself to be touched by them or their world is the only objective and scientific attitude. It is not only Christ who remains unintelligible to this attitude; whole stretches of the world of even natural things are shut out from our minds, if we regard them merely passively from outside, instead of going out to meet them with the reverence due to them. This neutralism ends in a drab ideal of knowledge, for it fears to be biased as soon as it begins to be moved or carried along by the object in question—in other words, as soon as a real contact with it is made. In ethics this deformation of knowledge produces utilitarianism; in the theory of knowledge, pragmatism; in life, the attitude of the Boeotian and materialist; in art, the ideal of the "new objectivity." It is also partly responsible for Bolshevism. The cosmos, illuminated as it is by value, demands an affective response; in its degradation to a mere network of ends lies one of the deepest roots of the Bolshevist attitude.

We are now in a position to understand the profound deformations of knowledge which may occur in various types of mind, and the connection between such types, as well as the generic form of man on the one side and his capacity for knowledge on the other, and the deeper dependence of knowledge on the fundamental attitude.

A more careful analysis has shown us that, in order to attain to a knowledge which is to be unprejudiced—i.e., purely objective, determined by the object and not by our wishes and prejudices—it is not sufficient merely to abstain consciously from all presuppositions concerning the object. Such knowledge demands further the right attitude of the person in order to secure for knowledge a clear run, freedom from dimming interferences. But here it becomes evident that the objectivity of the modern university is more appearance than fact. It is a self-delusion: because people are not *consciously* aware of prejudices as such, they imagine that *therefore* their knowledge is free, and that there are no other impediments, outside the sphere of knowledge perhaps, but nevertheless prejudging the result. We cannot remain satisfied with such a merely negative absence of prejudice; we demand more: namely, the positively unhampered and free exercise of knowledge which only the right fundamental attitude can guarantee.

In saying this I do not mean to depreciate the great and notable body of knowledge which has been the conquest of the modern university. The achievements in natural science, history, philology, medicine, law are in many respects admirable and praiseworthy. At the same time, many have been the one-sided and erroneous results that have sprung from that same soil, such as Darwinism or historicism. Above all, it becomes intelligible how precisely in the sphere of philosophy, despite the utmost intelligence, industry, and erudition, unheard-of platitudes and the most arrant nonsense have been dished up with solemn scientific pretensions, such as materialism, relativism, skepticism, positivism, the mechanistic association-psychology, and many other theories. Not infrequently the fundamental attitude has obscured knowledge to such an extent that, in spite of unquestionable intelligence, plainly silly assertions have been propounded.

If we now raise the question, what is the specifically Catholic attitude to the world of reality—i.e., the attitude created by Catholic dogma in a person who lives in a world such as is opened to us by Revelation and represented in the community of the Church—the answer is that it is precisely the fundamental attitude that *delivers* our knowledge, clears away all the fetters and hindrances to knowledge, and so produces the type of mind capable of doing justice to the depth and range of reality. The Catholic attitude is specifically soaring, specifically anti-pedantic, anti-self-complacent, open-minded, filled with respect for reality. The Catholic conception of the world is such that anyone who fixes his glance upon it and surrenders himself to it must necessarily possess this soaring, this yearning, open, and reverent mind. The Catholic world is a cosmos ruled by an all-good, all-powerful, omniscient God who has created all, for whom all exists, who comprises all in infinite love, who has united us by and in Christ with Himself supernaturally and has implanted in us His own divine life with baptism, and has called us to sanctity and eternal beatitude with Himself; has given us the possibility through and by and with Christ to worship Him and sacrifice to Him adequately, and has united us among ourselves in a supernatural communion of Love, communion of merits and prayers. Can we conceive anything more patently antithetical to a mediocre, smug, diminutive picture of the world or the commonplace ideal of the "New Objectivity" of a world without values?

The true Catholic is, to quote St. Bonaventure again, "a man of desire like Daniel," and the true Catholic attitude is one of humility, free from all *ressentiment*, ready to submit and to serve; it is metaphysically courageous, healthy, un-disgruntled, *believing*. I say this is the *Catholic attitude, not* the attitude of the average Catholic. We may indeed be told, not without justification, that many Catholic men of science and erudition show a lack of this attitude more than many non-Catholics. If we think of some of the great men of antiquity, Socrates, Plato, Aristotle, or those of modern times, such as Kepler, Newton, Robert Mayer, Leibnitz, Humboldt, we find that they were, in their fundamental attitude, far more "Catholic" than many a Catholic. How much smugness and pedantry, how much metaphysical indolence do we not find among Catholics and Catholic thinkers and men of science! Certainly; but not because they are Catholics; rather because they are *not Catholic enough,* because their attitude has not been formed by dogma, because dogma has not become a principle of their life, so that the attitude they display does not fully correspond with what they affirm in their Faith. Where, on the contrary, this is the case, as with St. Augustine, St. Anselm, St. Bonaventure, St. Albertus Magnus, St. Thomas, Pascal, Père Gratry, Cardinal Newman, or Giambattista Rossi, Vico, Toniolo, Pasteur —there we also find that fundamental attitude which delivers knowledge and opens the way for it.

There is a wide difference between a Catholic scientist or thinker and a scientist and thinker who is incidentally also a Catholic. A large number of Catholic men of science have allowed the modern university to force on them the ideal of its pseudo freedom from prejudice. They think that they must forget that they are Catholics as soon as they take up their science, in order to work without bias in their research. They surrender thereby the tremendous start that they possess as Catholics in the way of genuine freedom, and assume in its stead an attitude impeding and darkening their outlook. I naturally presuppose a *material* freedom from prejudice and a clear distinction between the *lumen naturale* (natural knowledge) and the *lumen supranaturale* of Revelation. The Catholic thinker, pursuing natural studies, must sharply distinguish between what he knows by Revelation and what is accessible to natural reason. But neither should he forget what he knows by Revelation, for, if Revelation and natural reason represent two distinct paths to truth, there is yet objectively but *one* Truth, which cannot be self-contradictory. If a contradiction results between revealed truth and that yielded by natural reason, the Catholic will, of course, consider such contradiction as merely apparent, since he is convinced that the *lumen naturale,* which after all is also from God, cannot, provided it is allowed to shine without hindrance, lead to a contradiction with the *lumen supranaturale.* He will trust the *lumen supranaturale.* But he will not rush into the assertion that his natural knowledge demonstrates something which in fact it has not yet proved; he will continue his research, go more deeply into it, check everything all the more critically, until the apparent contradiction is solved. Cardinal Newman said:

> (The Catholic) is sure, and nothing shall make him doubt, that if anything seems to be proved by astronomer, or geologist, or chronologist, or antiquarian, or ethnologist, in contradiction to the dogmas of faith, that point will eventually turn out, first, *not* to be proved, or secondly, not *contradictory,* or thirdly, not contradictory to any thing *really* revealed, but to something which has been confused with revelation.[3]

What a warning against all superficial study this affirmation contains! What a salutary discipline, to go into things and get down to the bedrock of problems! What an incitement, instead of losing ourselves in one-sidedness, with our glance fixed on one single point of

[3] "Christianity and Scientific Investigation," *The Idea of a University* (London, 1923), pp. 466–67.

the universe, never to lose sight of the place our special field of study, however much we cultivate it, occupies within the general structure of reality! What a help to attain to the real *universitas* in the midst of all the errors of one-sided specialization! By all means let us appreciate the autonomous character of a special field; but it is an essential part of its very autonomy that it should occupy this particular place *in the whole.* The Catholic attitude will protect the researcher more than anything else against impatient, pedantic violations of the peculiar and autonomous nature of his special subject, and his reverent listening will prevent him from rushing into hasty systematizations. On the other hand, we can understand how easily a science, and especially a philosophy, resulting from knowledge dimmed or deformed by a false attitude, lapses into contradictions with the content of dogma, or rather with the natural truths which are implicitly presupposed by dogma, and then gives rise to materialism, psychologism, relativism, skepticism, idealism, Darwinism. But this is not a contradiction that results from knowledge having been given free course, without prejudice, without dogmatic hindrance, but is due rather to the fact that a genuinely unprejudiced, really objective knowledge was never reached, for it was impeded by a false attitude and never really made contact with things.

I hope that what I have said will not be misunderstood in the sense that all that is needed to reach adequate and valuable results in knowledge is to possess the right attitude. This is but one, even though a fundamental, prerequisite. Natural gifts and intelligence are of course also needed, both general intelligence and that particular kind specially required for special fields of knowledge. Such gifts are a gift of God, and being a Catholic is no guarantee of their possession. The utmost piety is no substitute for such talents, and nothing could be more foolish than a sense of superiority in this respect on the part of a Catholic. Neither will the right fundamental attitude dispense the Catholic from the full burden of methodical work, devoted thoroughness, and patient, critical application to research. Nor is he dispensed from consulting the results of non-Catholic work, or from appreciating and applying whatever has been obtained by it. All I mean here is that the right fundamental attitude is an essential and decisive factor; and that, moreover, without it no adequate knowledge is possible, however much other advantages of intelligence, industry, and thoroughness may be present.

For this reason the Catholic may never artificially divest himself, even in the use of his natural reason, of the attitude that the *lumen supranaturale* imparts to him; on the contrary, for the sake precisely of really unprejudiced, objective knowledge and genuinely scientific work, the Catholic cannot follow too much the guiding influence of Revelation in the formation of his fundamental attitude, cannot be too Catholic. *Catholic universities* are therefore necessary for the sake of truly adequate objective knowledge, not by any means merely for the protection of the religious convictions of the students. They are needed as the institutions where Catholic thinkers and men of science, supported by a truly Catholic environment, informed in their attitude by the spirit of Christ and of His Church, shall be enabled by a really unbiased, truly liberated and enlightened intelligence to penetrate adequately to reality and to achieve by organized teamwork that *universitas* which is nowadays so urgently needed. They must further be institutions in which young people may be educated to that attitude which represents an inevitable prerequisite for the learner also. A Catholic university would have no meaning if it were nothing but a collection of Catholic men of thought and science, while following the model of the modern university in its general atmosphere. It requires the conscious production of an atmosphere filled by Christ, an environment imbued with prayer; as an organism it must, in its structure and in the common life of its teachers among each other and with their students, be thoroughly Catholic. The students must breathe a Catholic air and Catholic spirit which will make them into anti-pedantic, humble, faithful, metaphysically courageous men of winged intelligence and yearning, and therewith capable of truly adequate and objective knowledge. The demand for a Catholic university must therefore be pressed in the name of such adequate knowledge and not by any means only in the interest of Catholics.

It does not follow that Catholics should abandon the present universities to their fate and that all Catholic teachers and students should be concentrated in Catholic universities alone. It is rather with the help of Catholic universities, as the homes of a really liberating attitude, that the baneful spell of the pseudo-freedom from prejudice may be broken which hypnotizes non-

Catholic universities and fetters Catholic teachers therein. Only through the existence of Catholic universities can the labors of Catholic research in the other universities be brought to full fruition. Catholic universities must create the atmosphere in which the Catholic teacher can find his way back to a true ideal of science and become conscious of the advantage for adequate knowledge which he enjoys through revelation, and of the responsibility of giving to mankind in the way of knowledge what by reason of this advantage he is capable of giving to it.

Similarly, the demand for Catholic universities does not imply that Catholics should not frequent non-Catholic universities. If the Catholic student has the material possibility of going to a Catholic university, he will prefer it to a non-Catholic institution, although even then nothing stands in the way of his studying temporarily there also, especially if his subject makes it desirable. But in the absence of the material possibility of frequenting a Catholic university, he will go, as hitherto, to a non-Catholic place of study: he will, however, find even there the spirit of the Catholic university in the instruction of Catholic teachers who have set themselves free from the illusions of a pseudo-freedom from prejudice. Finally, the effect of the Catholic university is not meant to be limited to Catholics only. The liberation of knowledge by an attitude of freedom, humility, and courage will grip also the non-Catholic man of science and thus help to regenerate the spirit of the other universities as well. The Catholic university is not intended as a sort of "ghetto" for Catholics, but as the nursery of this liberating attitude and the fortress of adequate knowledge, of that attitude which must permeate like a leaven all truly scientific knowledge and study.

I turn in conclusion to another aspect of the Catholic university; namely, to the features it should present as a community of students and teachers. The function of the student in the university is naturally that of receptivity and of the acquisition of knowledge. If nowadays the demand is often made that students should have more influence on the shaping of the university, that they should be treated less like pupils, that lectures should be replaced by co-operation in study, a Catholic university must insist on the willingness of the student really to learn and to accept instruction. The years of study must, after all, be a period of growth, of absorption, and the real work must consist in the assimilation of what the student is taught.

Per contra, a Catholic university will display nothing of that professional superiority that removes the teacher to an Olympian distance from the student. The teacher, too, must be possessed of that humble attitude which alone enables him to discharge the high and responsible office of searching for and proclaiming the truth. He must stand toward the student, not in a position of schoolmasterly superiority, but of affectionate guidance, informed by a sense of fellowship springing from the bond of service to God in the pursuit of truth.

For the Catholic university must neither as a whole nor in its separate faculties be torn from the context of the whole of human destiny, nor must it become a place for the idolizing of science or for that modern heresy, the idolatry of the profession. It should rather, as a whole, bear witness to the true hierarchy of values, a principle which must dominate its smallest details. It must not prefer the absurd claim to be the focal point of the world; its teachers must not present the ridiculous figure of the typical professor, who considers the university as his world and, absorbed in his specialty, forgets to be a man, whose true destiny is to know and love God. The Catholic university as a whole must occupy its place in the cosmos of God and must not pretend to any other position than that which belongs to it in God's plan. Even though devoted wholly to knowledge, it must be inspired by the function and the real end of humanity, which is to glorify God by the sanctification of every man. It must be an institution whose atmosphere is impregnated by Christ and the whole wealth of values, so that the student, however much advanced in a special field of study may be his task in the university, yet remains free from the modern professional heresy that places man's center of gravity no longer in his love of God and his neighbor, but in his achievement in a definite profession, in which his person ranks lower than his achievement.[4]

The university must accordingly be a place in which, alongside of specialized studies, the true hierarchy of

[4] Cf. "Efficiency and Holiness," pp. 207 ff.

values is so cultivated as to be a fortress against infection by all those heresies, by all those idols and fetishes which at times poison the air of a period, as nowadays, for instance, nationalism, statolatry, racism, the biological materialism, and above all that divinization of achievement that stifles all deeper life, replaces virtue by efficiency, has nothing but recreation and amusement to set over against work, leaves no room for contemplation and meditation, makes man into a spiritual cripple and life into a perpetual escape from oneself, which is at bottom nothing but a flight from God.

No less must the university be the place where man never forgets that his primary function is to bring to full fruition that divine life implanted in him by Baptism, to imitate Christ, to radiate Christ. For, as stated at the beginning, knowledge will develop free and clear and penetrate the depth of things only in proportion as it is backed by the right attitude; but the right attitude means the full and complete man, open and responsive to the world of values, who lives *in conspectu Dei,* who lives because he loves. The words of Leonardo da Vinci, "The greater the man, the deeper his love," must not be forgotten in the university.

For that reason the Catholic university must insist on the transmission not only of specialized knowledge, but also of true general culture, and especially allow no student to leave its walls without a thorough religious education. For not even the most ardent devotion to one's profession can ever nullify the words of Christ:

"Martha, Martha, thou art careful, and art troubled about many things: but one thing is necessary."

Let us not delude ourselves with the belief that we can ever love a good with greater love than by leaving it in that place where it stands in the eyes of God. To love God more than all else means also to embrace each good in the deepest and truest love; only in proportion as we love God above all else and see everything *in conspectu Dei* can we even become capable of full, ardent love. The idolator loves the state, the nation, science, art, not more but less than he who is free from idolatry.

A spirit of freedom, such as only a life from and with Christ can give, must inspire the whole university and blow away all pedantry and caste spirit and tin-god service. The form of its life must be given not by an academic bureaucracy, but by the spirit of Christ and the universal spirit of Catholicism. This alone is right and appropriate for a place devoted to the search for and proclamation of truth. Away with the ideal of pseudo-objectivity, with the secularized atmosphere in which the name of Christ appears like an anachronism! Away with the false conception that man is the more capable of scientific study, the more sterile he is as man, the smaller his living contact is with the whole wealth of the world! Away with the fallacy that a pedantic, distanced neutrality is the true index of the scientific mind! Whatever a university achieves can be but a part of life as a whole. Knowledge, however great its value *per se,* must, as a whole, form an organic part of the destiny of the individual and of mankind.

The Catholic university means to give these matters their rightful place. It must be inspired by the spirit of Him to whom all our life, our intellect, our will, our love belong: *Christus heri, hodie et in saecula.*

Translated by Edward Bullough.

THE ROLE OF REVERENCE IN EDUCATION

REVERENCE can be rightly called "the mother of all virtues," as it is the basic attitude that all virtues presuppose. The most elementary gesture of reverence is a response to being as such, to the autonomous majesty of being as opposed to any mere illusion or fiction; it is a response to its inner consistency and positiveness, to its independence from our arbitrary mood. In reverence, we conform to this fundamental value of being and we appreciate it; we give to being the opportunity to unfold itself, as it were, to speak to us, to fecundate our mind. The basic attitude of reverence is, therefore, already indispensable for any adequate knowledge. The depth and plenitude of being, and, above all, its mysteries will never reveal themselves except to the reverent mind.

In the θαυμάζειν ("wondering") which Plato and Aristotle claimed to be the indispensable presupposition for philosophy, reverence is a constitutive element. Indeed, lack of reverence is one of the main sources of philosophical errors. But if reverence is a necessary basis for every true and adequate knowledge of being, it is, above all, indispensable for the grasping and understanding of values. Only to the reverent man, who is ready to admit the existence of something greater than himself, who is willing to be silent and let the object speak to him, who opens himself, will the sublime world of values disclose itself. This already explains why reverence is the mother of all virtues, as every virtue implies a superactual response to the value of a certain sphere of being and thus presupposes a grasping and understanding of values.

Again, the adequate response to being, the value of which has been grasped, contains an element of reverence, a new reverence responding not only to the value of being as such, but to the specific value of a certain being and to its rank in the hierarchy of values. This new reverence opens our eyes for a discovery of ever newer values.

Thus reverence is on one hand a presupposition for our grasping and understanding of values, and, on the other, an essential element of the adequate value-response. It is, therefore, a necessary condition and an essential part of all virtues. Man seems to take into account his essentially receptive character as a created person in the reverent attitude alone. The ultimate grandeur of man is to be *capax Dei*. We can enlarge on this and say that man has the capacity to grasp something greater than himself, to be affected and fecundated by it, to abandon himself to it for its own sake in a pure value-response. It is the essential transcendence of man which distinguishes him from a plant or an animal that strives exclusively to unfold its own entelechy. Only the reverent man conforms consciously to man's fundamental condition and to his metaphysical situation. He takes toward being the attitude that alone actualizes his receptive capacity to be fecundated by something greater than himself.

The irreverent man who approaches being either in an attitude of arrogant superiority or of a tactless, smug familiarity has incapacitated himself for an adequate knowledge and understanding of the depth and mysteries of being and especially for the perception of values. He behaves like a man who comes so near to a tree or a building that he can no longer see it. Instead of remaining at the spiritual distance from the object which reverence implies, and maintaining a reverent silence, allowing being to speak its word, he obtrudes himself upon being by constant, loud, and bombastic talk.

Reverence plays a specific role in the realm of purity. Purity essentially involves a reverent attitude toward the mystery of love between man and woman, a consciousness that the sphere of sex is a realm which should fill us with awe and which should be approached only with a special sanction from God. Purity is incompatible with a general arrogant attitude toward being, whether it assumes a frivolous, cynical character or a blunt, smug familiarity with the mysteries of the cosmos.

Purity demands respect for the beloved, respect for his body, respect for the great, mysterious union of two souls in one flesh, respect for the mystery of the "becoming" of a new human being.

In the education that fosters purity, the role of the general attitude of reverence cannot be overestimated. We cannot expect of a young man a right attitude in the domain of sex if we neglect to nourish in him reverence in general.

Before we analyze more in detail the means to the formation of reverence we must briefly examine the specific obstacles to such an education—obstacles due partly to the age of puberty, partly to the mentality of our modern epoch. The adolescent between fifteen and eighteen years of age, especially the boy, is endangered by an attitude we could call the hysteria of independence and bluff. He craves independence and, above all, he wants to impress other people with his independence and superiority. He refuses to admit that anything moves him, fills him with respect, impresses or surprises him. He strives to play the role of the "independent man" who sees through everything, who is above all things, and who displays an unshakable security. But, in truth, his desire to display this security is proportionate to his insecurity. Actually, he is completely dependent upon others, and even in an illegitimate way. He indiscriminately copies those people who impress him by their so-called virility, independence, and superiority, and who precisely make him feel his own insecurity. He hopes to acquire their independence and security by copying them in everything. It is the type which Dostoevski has so masterfully described in *The Idiot* and in *The Brothers Karamazov*. This mixture of inferiority complex, of being not yet completely adult, and of the desire to give the impression of being so, this combination of pride and insecurity, this specific immaturity pervaded by a boasting tendency, is clearly an antithesis to reverence. In such a state of mind one sees in any reverent approach to something a loss of independent virility and superiority, and the young man dominated by it is eager to exhibit a "nothing sacred" attitude toward all those things that call for a reverent approach, for submission and respect. He is inclined to speak irreverently about the Church, about moral obligations, about marriage, about love.

This general danger in the adolescent is one of the great obstacles with which the task of forming reverence is confronted.

The other main obstacle is the irreverent trend in the mentality of our modern epoch. Man no longer wants to accept his character of a creature, to admit the fundamental *religio* toward something that is above him. He refuses to submit to obligations not created by his free commitment, to look respectfully at great goods such as marriage, children, his own life. He does not want to accept toward these goods the role of a mere administrator, but, on the contrary, he arrogates an arbitrary sovereignty over them.

We saw before that the modern man no longer wants to admit the role of Providence in his life, but wants to determine everything himself; he strives for a life without gifts, without surprise, in which everything occurring to him is according to a schedule he himself has fixed. He even considers it desirable to be able to change his sex at will. The climax of this repulsive irreverence and criminal sovereignty is reached in artificial insemination.

This modern attempt to cast off our human condition as creatures and to deny our metaphysical situation is obviously antithetical to reverence. This mentality, which finds its philosophical expression in Sartre's existentialism, penetrates into the most minute differentiations of modern life, and the young man inhales the germs of irreverence with every breath. The progressing utilitarianism and pragmatism of our daily life, the devaluation of space and time by our modern techniques, the "overdimensioning" of man's life, destroy the consciousness of an autonomous reality imposing itself on us, and foster an unhealthy consciousness of an unlimited sovereignty on the part of man. The corrosion of the reverent attitude occurs in many cases through channels the danger of which the Catholic educator overlooks, or rather which he does not recognize in their destructive function with regard to reverence. He does, indeed, deplore evils such as divorces, birth control, euthanasia, the frequent suicides, the growing shamelessness in relations between the two sexes; but often perhaps he may not realize in the first place the role of irreverence as a root of these evils, or he may recognize the role of irreverence, but only so long as disrespect of God or of moral values is at stake. He is not aware, however, how many elements in our modern life foster the attitude of irreverence to things apparently not related to religion and morality.

Such elements are, for instance, the modern attitude toward art and beauty in general, the entire tendency of neglecting forms, of taking it easy and letting ourselves go, and last, but not least, our own language, our slovenly way of expressing ourselves.

The modern man no longer approaches beauty in nature and art with reverence, as something reflecting a higher world above him. He makes no effort to prepare himself for a real understanding of a great work of art; he shuns the *sursum corda* that is required if we are to be moved and fecundated by a great work of art. He wants beauty to be offered to him on a dish, so that he may relish it while relaxing physically and mentally. He treats great works of art as a source of fun, and does not shrink from changing them *ad libitum,* arranging a quartet for orchestra, a novel for the movies. This attitude toward the sphere of aesthetic values, neutral and innocent as it may seem at a superficial glance from the moral and religious point of view, is in reality a disastrous phenomenon of increasing irreverence. Man is a whole, and once irreverence corrodes one sphere of his life, his entire personality becomes affected by it. Irreverence and spiritual laziness, which is closely linked to it, the refusal to make a spiritual effort in order to acquire a real contact with a great work of art or to appreciate sublime beauty in nature, the unwillingness to create the indispensable recollection, to emerge from the periphery and the things that appeal to our superficial side—all these are poisonous germs that also manifest themselves in our moral and religious life.

The same applies to the modern attitude toward

exterior forms in general. Greeting other persons by shaking their hands or by lifting our hat is a deep expression of the call to direct ourselves in an outspoken act toward the other person as such before we turn to any other topic in talking to him. To substitute for it "hello," which suggests the casual, *en passant* attitude, or to drop it completely, is a typical symptom of irreverence toward our neighbors and of a mood of smug familiarity, of letting ourselves go.

The camaraderie in the relation between the two sexes replacing the chivalrous attitude that responds to the mystery of femininity, and the lack of politeness, which is misunderstood as a "sissified" and superfluous attitude, are equally symptoms of irreverence. Let us not overlook the undermining influence implicit in such a neglect of exterior forms—a neglect that affects even our very carriage, our *tenue,* and the rhythm of vitality in our bodily behavior. It is not in vain that the liturgy insists on a proper bodily attitude in praying, that St. Benedict lays such weight on the bearing of the monk, which should breathe reverence and a *habitare secum,* and form an antithesis to any kind of slovenliness. Exterior behavior is not only an expression of the inner attitude, but it also has an influence on our inner attitude, and facilitates at least the engendering of the inner attitude of reverence.

Two factors are at the basis of this deterioration of form in our modern life: the utilitarian, pragmatic approach that considers as a pompous embellishment everything not strictly indispensable for the attainment of a certain end, and the idol of comfort, the unrestrained pursuit of the "easier way" which entails the least bodily and mental strain.

But it would be erroneous to consider a lack of virility and self-control responsible for this idol of comfort. Our modern times excel, on the contrary, in great sporting records, and physical education is now much stressed. It is the irreverent, proud attitude that shuns any effort, especially any spiritual strain which issues from a call of the value of an object instead of being arbitrarily chosen by us. At the basis of this decay of form is the rejection of the *habitare secum,* and the refusal to display modesty and recollection in our exterior behavior—factors that are, therefore, much more serious than mere lack of discipline. A training imposed merely from without (as in military discipline) can never overcome the evil. Rather, it is necessary to awaken the sense for exterior forms as adequate expressions of the inner attitude of reverence, modesty, and *discretio.* It is necessary, moreover, to help us to persevere in this inner attitude.

Moreover, the way in which we express ourselves, the way in which we speak of great and sublime things, is above all a channel through which the corrosion of our reverent attitude takes place. And here the religious educator himself is often guilty.

In an unfortunate though well-intentioned desire to make the sphere of religion familiar to us, to bring it close to the people, he translates the sublime, supernatural world into trite terms that undermine *discretio* and reverence. Instead of following the pattern of the liturgy, which approaches divine things with words filled with an atmosphere of sublime reverence, elevating us above our own pettiness, drawing us into the *lumen Christi,* appealing to a *sursum corda* on our part, he speaks about divine things, as it were, in slang. Let us not fool ourselves. Though we stress again and again the necessity of reverence toward God and the entire supernatural and religious sphere in our education, if we do it in terms which breathe irreverence, which introduce a smug familiarity toward God, we simultaneously desubstantialize that which we want to build up in the soul of the young person. We then defeat our own purpose.

In view of the above-mentioned obstacles, we can only hope to engender and maintain reverence in the young man by surrounding him with an atmosphere of reverence toward all those things that deserve a reverent approach, by refraining from any language and expression that smack of irreverence, by abstaining from all compromises with the manifold modern manifestations of irreverence, by confronting him with a style of life that is deeply formed by reverence.

Furthermore, we should cautiously abstain from making any compromise with the previously described hysteria of independence and bluff. The educator must not use a slovenly jargon in order to give young men the feeling of being understood. Rather, he should strive on every occasion to dissolve this cramp, this imprisonment in human respect, by ridiculing this pseudo-virility and the fear of being considered a "sissy."

The ideal of impressing others by one's independence and superiority should again and again be unmasked as a result of complete dependence upon the opinion of others, as a fruit of cowardice before human respect, as an unobjective imprisonment with one's own person. We should time and again present to the young the grandeur of humility, of contrition, of obedience, the true freedom that only the reverent and humble person possesses. We should be aware of the danger of fostering their virility-idol by overstressing self-control *for its own sake,* and by appealing to their honor as a motive for morality. The fear of manifesting any emotion—the attitude that considers tears, regardless of their character and of their source, as something to be ashamed of—should not only never be encouraged but, on the contrary, should be fought. There is no doubt that the virility-idol is sometimes encouraged and used as a means to obtain certain results. The immediate end may be attained in this way, but in the long run the motive so used in order to avoid some immediate dangers will prove disastrous.

Let us exemplify this general task in a more detailed way with respect to purity. We already mentioned the fundamental role of reverence in purity. We dare say that most sins committed today against the sixth commandment are due not to overflowing vitality and indomitable instincts but to a lack of reverence. Awakening of the reverent attitude toward the mystery embraced by the sphere of sex is one of the great factors in the education that is to nourish purity. This concerns, first, the way in which one makes the child acquainted with this sphere. Every neutralizing interpretation that presents this sphere primarily from a biological, scientific point of view is incapable of engendering the attitude of reverence. On the contrary, it rather destroys the sense for the mystery implied in this mysterious realm. Neither can such an interpretation succeed in silencing the specific attraction of this realm by substituting a neutral aspect for its dangerous charm, as is thematic in medicine; nor is this aspect even desirable from the moral and religious point of view. It would be an attempt to overcome the moral danger of impurity from below instead of from above, an approach that is always wrong. Thus the merely biological, neutral way of dealing with the sphere of sex not only bypasses the moral dangers of this realm by sacrificing its true and authentic aspect and favoring an undesirable attitude, but, secondly, is even an ineffective means of preserving purity.

This sphere must, on the contrary, be presented to the child in the light of its spiritual content, upon the child's having reached the right age, and when it becomes an indispensable necessity to acquaint him with certain facts. It must be interpreted as a mysterious expression of an ultimate love between man and woman and as an ultimate union which, because of its depth and beauty, cannot be approached without a specific sanction from God. It must be presented in the light of marriage, of its sacramental character, of its analogy to Christ's relation to the Church. On the background of the beauty of the God-given meaning of this sphere in its intimate union with love and being in love, the necessity of remaining at a respectful distance from it must be stressed.

A respect for the grandeur and depth of this mystery in its God-given place, an understanding of the positive value here at stake, are alone able to disclose the *mysterium iniquitatis* that accompanies any abuse of this sphere. We should not speak to young people of the sex sphere in terms that make it seem the devil's own territory—but that is what we do when we begin by stressing merely the sinfulness that any illegitimate actualization of it involves. Such an approach could never become the basis for the true virtue of purity. Above all, how could anything intrinsically negative be elevated to the dignity of a sacrament? On the contrary, only in presenting this domain as something mysteriously great in its function as an ultimate mutual self-donation, a becoming two in one flesh, does the loathsomeness of every isolation of this domain for its own sake become clear, as well as the sinfulness of every approach to it without the express sanction of God.

Our end must be not to deprive this sphere of its mysterious character and neutralize its seductive danger with a scientific presentation, but to engrave in the souls of young people awe and respect for it, to lead them to consider it as a *hortus conclusus* until God calls them, in marriage, to set foot in this mysterious land.

BEAUTY IN THE LIGHT OF THE REDEMPTION

WHAT IMPORTANCE is to be attributed to beauty in the life of a Christian? What role *should* it play in the life of those who have been redeemed? What is the relationship between Redemption and beauty? Did beauty lose its significance after the Redemption?

We can use the term beauty in a more general sense and in a more specific one. When we are profoundly affected by the beauty of purity, when the Church in her liturgy exclaims: "How beautiful is the chaste generation with splendor," or, again, when we speak of the beauty acquired by a soul through humility, then we are concentrating on a beauty that is an aura, a refulgence, a radiance of the inner value of these virtues. It is a beauty which St. Augustine calls *splendor veri*, and which is, as it were, a radiation of every genuine value that inheres in a good to the extent that it possesses value. Beauty in this sense will be termed *ontological beauty*.[1]

This beauty is not our problem here. Its relationship

[1] By ontological beauty I refer neither to the general value of being, nor to beauty as transcendental; nor do I mean an ontological value in contradistinction to a qualitative one. Cf. D. von Hildebrand, *Christian Ethics*, chap. 10.

Beauty is always a qualitative value. By ontological beauty I refer to the qualitative value that is rooted in every other qualitative or ontological value, as its efflorescence or fragrance. The term *ontological* beauty is intended to stress the difference between this type of beauty and form beauty—i.e., the beauty of visible and audible things. Cf. D. von Hildebrand, *Zum Wesen der Schoenheit des Sichtbaren und Hoerbaren* (Brussels, 1950).

to the Redemption, its function in the life of the Christian, is not problematic. The liturgy leaves no doubt in our minds as to the role due to this beauty in the light of revelation. Again and again it is spoken of in a great variety of phrases, as for example:

> Listen, daughter, and see, and incline thine ear,
> for the king has greatly desired thy beauty.
>
> Give ear with thy countenance and thy beauty.
>
> Beautiful in countenance and more beautiful
> in faith.

There are many similar references in the liturgy. This beauty is not to be severed from the value whose reflection and aura it is. Therefore, it naturally has a conspicuous function in the life of the Christian, for this beauty is the foundation of love. The divine beauty of Jesus, the beauty of the Saint of all saints, inflames our heart. It shone resplendent on the apostles on Tabor; the beauty of His divine mercy melted the heart of Mary Magdalen. The irresistible divine beauty of Jesus not only moves our will, but it attracts our heart; as St. Augustine says, "We are attracted not only by the will but also by delight."

The great Lacordaire says that virtues become irresistibly victorious and constrain us to love only when, as in every saint, they are manifested in their beauty, when their inner nobility is revealed in their beauty. This beauty is a radiation of the inner "preciousness" as well as of the qualitative values with which this being is endowed. Thus, this beauty depends in its rank on the object, and on the rank of the qualitative values it is able to embody. The beauty of a rich, profound mind like that of Plato or Aristotle is greater than the beauty of an Achilles, which is peculiar to the vital fullness of an exuberant vigor; and the beauty of humility or love is greater than that of an eminent and profound intellect. When we contemplate objects endowed with this beauty, we can even say that beauty is never their true primary theme.

The beauty of humility is not the primary theme of humility, just as the beauty of truth is not the primary theme of truth. It is an exuberance, yet connected essentially with these values, an efflorescence of them, the perfume of their essence, their "countenance." Therefore, it is so much a part of Redemption, that Redemption is also a restoration of the original paradisaical beauty, of an even much greater beauty, as the liturgy maintains: "Who has wonderfully created human dignity and more wonderfully restored it," and as a mystic says: "We would die of love if we could see the beauty of a soul in the state of grace."

Our problem, however, is that of beauty in a narrower sense of the word, of beauty that radiates from visible and audible things. It is the beauty that unfolds before us when we look out from the Capitoline Hill upon the Roman Forum with the Campagna and the Alban Hill in the distance, or the beauty of the Medicean monuments by Michelangelo, or the beauty revealed when we listen to Beethoven's Ninth Symphony. It is the beauty of the visible and the audible with which we are confronted in nature and in art, and which, for want of another expression, we shall call the beauty of form by way of contrast with ontological beauty.

What is the relationship of *this* beauty to the Redemption? What is its status in the life of the Christian? What importance is due to it in the light of revelation and of our transformation in Christ? Some maintain: "Beauty of form belongs to the sphere of luxury, to that part of life which, in the light of Christ, cannot lay claim to belong to the serious aspect of life. Certainly it is nothing wicked; it is something innocent. The question whether a building is beautiful or not, whether there is one work of art more or less, is really something secondary and external. For esthetes and pagans it may seem like something great and important; for the Christian who, with holy sobriety, knows that the serious things of life are to be sought in the moral and social fields, beauty of form is something relatively trifling and unserious. Certainly it belongs to human life as do amusements and games of every kind. It is, however, much more important that a knife cut well than that it look beautiful. It is more important that a person have a roof over his head than that his house merely satisfy an exquisitely artistic taste. Art, the whole culture related to beauty of form, is something only for the upper ten thousand, after all. This consideration in itself proves that beauty of form is something that does not really belong to the seriousness of existence. In former ages of princely courts and of feudal organizations, the whole cult of the beautiful flourished; our times are too serious for that. Today the Christian must concentrate upon great economic, political, and social problems. Love of neighbor must show him that it is much more important for every person to maintain an existence worthy of a human being, that the sick and the poor must be cared for, than that a beautiful painting exists some place or other or that *Figaro* be brilliantly performed. The same criterion applies to churches. Of importance are the tabernacle, the altar, the Holy Sacrifice celebrated there, for which an abode must be provided. Whether or not this abode be artistically beautiful is secondary. Only esthetes can find this essential."

In other words, in the minds of these individuals beauty of form in the light of Christ is something unessential and destitute of genuine seriousness; so much so, that this beauty threatens to weaken us, to make sensualists of us, to turn us away from the real duties of a Christian and from those things which, from the viewpoint of Christian charity, are indispensable. In the life of the Christian it should, therefore, play a quite secondary role.

Respondeo:

This utilitarianism is by no means the spirit of the Gospel. Certainly, in the light of the *unum necessarium,* our eternal salvation, beauty of form is secondary, but this is equally true of economic and social problems. Does not Our Lord say, "Therefore be not solicitous saying, what shall we eat or what shall we drink or wherewith shall we be clothed?" In the light of the

Gospel, then, it is not possible to play off the "useful" and practically obligatory things of life against the beautiful by emphasizing the fact that beauty of form does not belong to the *unum necessarium,* for this is also valid for the sphere of the "useful." It is, rather, of consequence to understand that practical and absolute necessity is not the only standard for the value of things. Christ's saying, "Man does not live by bread alone," is to be applied, in the first place, to the religious sphere. It can, however, also be justly extended to every spiritual realm.

An estimate of all things from the viewpoint of their practical and absolute necessity, or restriction to that which is absolutely necessary—a spirit that is legitimately master of the technical sciences—is to be found neither in God's creation nor in the revelation of Christ. In these, on the contrary, the principle of superabundance rules. Is God not lavish in His creation? Do we not meet this divine profusion in the realm of propagation? Is beauty in nature not the clearest proof of this divine profusion, since it is in no way practically indispensable in the economy of nature? Is creation itself, as such, not the fruit of this divine profusion? Is it not the pure emanation of the infinite love of God and in no way necessary? The first miracle of Christ at the wedding feast of Cana reveals to us in a glorious manner the superabundance of divine love, which shows no restriction to that which is necessary. The wine was not at all indispensable for the wedding feast. It was not even entirely wanting, but there was simply lacking a sufficiency. Certainly the primary meaning of this miracle was the manifestation of Christ's divinity. Yet, does not the fact that the content of the miracle has reference only to heightening the resplendence of the feast imply a radical renunciation of all forms of utilitarianism? And when Our Lord says, "The poor you have always with you, but Me you have not always," may we not discover in His words a Magna Charta for the importance that should be conceded to beauty? Is the ointment, whose waste was criticized by the apostles, not an exalted symbol of the things which, without being indispensable, are yet good and pleasing to God? No, the indispensability of a thing is *one* point of view, the value of a thing another. The fact that beauty of form is not indispensable does not affect its value and its seriousness. Later we shall speak of the deep significance that dwells in beauty of form.

Sometimes, however, we hear objections to beauty of form which are to be taken more seriously. Certain individuals say: "Form beauty is something external, something that inheres in material and corporeal objects, to that which is visible and audible. It is, therefore, much more external and less sublime, to say the least, than ontological beauty that inheres in spiritual things—for example, the beauty of truth or of virtue, as we have mentioned above. No one can deny that beauty of form is something that belongs to the realm of the senses, and is for that reason necessarily something relatively inferior within the compass of the hierarchy of beings. May it, for this reason, still claim to have an important function in the life of the Christian? Does not all asceticism strive toward a detachment from the senses, to draw us back more and more into our spiritual nature, to become indifferent to that which pleases the senses and to advance beyond? Does not this beauty of form, therefore, also belong to the specially mundane things which, without being evil, yet divert us from God, from the Kingdom of God, and from our eternal destiny? For the mystic, much becomes sweet that was bitter to the senses, and much bitter that was sweet to the senses. Does it not belong to the revolution of revelation, to the new eyes with which we are to behold everything according to the Redemption, that this beauty of form loses its significance, that it proves to be one of the *vanitates* of the earth, as we read in the Book of Wisdom: "Appearance is deceitful and beauty is vain."

Would it not follow that this beauty is something especially mundane? In itself, it is something absolutely positive, nothing wicked; yet, is it not perishable, attached to the perishable? Is it not something that loses its significance the more we are united with God, the more we live in Christ "through Him, with Him and in Him"? Does not Our Lord say to Martha, "Martha, Martha, thou art careful, and art troubled about many things: but one thing is necessary"? (Luke 10:41–2.) Is this not also valid in the case of beauty of form in nature and art? For a pagan who recognizes only natural goods, whose mind is entirely directed toward earthly things, this beauty may be the goal; for him, however, who has been illuminated by the light of Christ, it can no longer be essential. Neither is sense for this beauty indispensable for sanctity. Form beauty cannot stand the test before the question of St. Aloysius, "What does this avail for eternity?" Should we not admit, then, that it is rather an obstacle in the process of dying to ourselves and of being transformed in Christ, and that it has, consequently, lost its significance through the Redemption?"

Respondeo:

This opinion is erroneous, and the error can be attributed to a many-faceted misunderstanding of the essence of beauty of form. Granted, this beauty inheres in visible and audible things. The comprehension of this beauty presupposes the use of the senses. A blind person cannot grasp the beauty of Bernini's Colonnade or that of the Church of San Marco in Venice. A deaf person cannot be moved by Beethoven's *Missa Solemnis* or by one of his quartets. Yet the point that matters here is to understand the function of the senses as well as the relationship of these visible and audible objects to their beauty. Although beauty of form presupposes sight and hearing, yet in itself it is by no means something belonging to the realm of the senses—something, as it were, connatural with this realm bearing the stamp of the corporeal-sensible. In the opinion mentioned above, beauty of form was spoken of as if it were a pleasurable sensation of the eye and the ear. That is manifestly a gross error. If a light blinds me, my senses experience displeasure, yet no one will say that this light is ugly or in bad taste. If I behold something indistinctly or with great effort, perhaps with spectacles that are no good, then this is a displeasure for my eyes, but that which I see does not necessarily thereby become ugly;

when I put on good spectacles and experience the clear and distinct vision as a pleasure, nevertheless that which I see can be ugly, base, or trivial, and appear to me to be so. The same is true for the ear. That which is pleasant or unpleasant to the senses is congenial with the sphere of the senses; it bears the stamp of the unspiritual, exterior, and not, however, of beauty or ugliness, which are clearly distinct from these sense experiences. The pleasure and the displeasure of my eyes are experienced in connection with my body; it is a sense experience. The beauty of the Palazzo Farnese, however, certainly has nothing to do with my body, and its comprehension is separated by a world from sensation.

It is also characteristic that beauty of form be found only in the realm of the visible and audible and not in the sphere of smell, taste, and touch. Even though we can certainly discern not only the difference between pleasant and unpleasant in the realm of smell, taste, and touch, but also more subtle qualities like commonplace, rich, or delicate, still, we cannot speak here of beauty in the full sense of the word; for beauty does not inhere in mere sense data, but in definite visible and audible entities which, even as such, represent something much more differentiated, more richly constructed and formed. Fragrances cannot fashion a new entity as tones do a melody. Briefly, beauty of form is not sensuous like the agreeable taste of food, and it does not, therefore, bear the stamp of the corporeal like these.

It is not sufficient, however, to distinguish beauty of form from the sensation of pleasure in the senses; within this beauty itself we must make some important distinctions.

ʊʊʊʊʊʊʊʊʊʊʊʊ

There are two kinds of beauty of form. One of them is comparatively primitive, as, for example, the beauty of a circle as opposed to an arbitrarily irregular figure, the beauty of a clear musical note as opposed to a noise, a chord as opposed to a discord, or the beauty of certain faces with regular features, let us say "Hollywood-beauty." This beauty, though it is no mere pleasure for the eyes, is still comparatively close to the world of the senses. The other is an immeasurably higher one. It demands not only the co-ordination of many more factors but, qualitatively, it is something entirely new. It is the beauty that unfolds before us when, on a glorious day, we look out from the Janiculum upon Rome and the mountains beyond, or when we contemplate the *Creation of Adam* by Michelangelo in the Sistine Chapel, or when we are absorbed by the sublime beauty in Mozart's *Don Giovanni*. Wherever *this* beauty appears, we are confronted with a whole spiritual world that is laden with a host of spiritual elements; the poetic as opposed to the prosaic, necessity as opposed to arbitrariness, inner abundance as opposed to every boring emptiness, genuineness and truth as opposed to falsehood and affectation, inner greatness as opposed to everything mediocre, breadth and depth as opposed to all that is insipid and flat.

Our problem has reference to this sublimely higher beauty of form, which so evidently rises above the world of the sensuous and discloses a sublime spirituality, and about which it is impossible to say that it is directed to the lower part of our soul. What is the position of *this* beauty of form with reference to the Redemption?

Attempts have not been wanting to rescue the spirituality of this beauty of form by maintaining that it is not in any way attached to the visible and audible: ideas or thoughts to which the audible and visible stimulates us are the true bearers of this beauty. If, for example, we view a lofty mountain range bathed in gleaming sunlight, it is not what we see directly before us to which beauty is attached; the thought of God's creative power is the real beauty. In a word, the real bearer of beauty is something spiritual which we connect intellectually with the visible and audible by means of analogies; or, it is said, the visible has a function similar to that of the symbol in the liturgy.

This attempt to rescue the spirituality of beauty is well-meant, to be sure, but it is false, for the beauty of the Campagna Romana or that of the Seventh Symphony by Bruckner is intuitively given, linked directly with that which is seen and heard, and no intellectual ascent to something else is necessary in order to grasp this beauty. We must not try to evade the mysteries in reality, but in a complete "wondering" (θαυμάζειν) at the mystery we must try to understand it by means of a deeper penetration. This higher beauty of form is also bestowed directly and intuitively by means of the visible and the audible; and in spite of its connection with the senses, it is of a spiritual sublimity which in quality completely transcends the sphere of the senses. How can this be explained?

This beauty (and we here arrive at one of the most important points) adheres directly to the visible and audible, to be sure, but it is not the *expression of the essence* of these visible and audible objects as is ontological beauty—for instance, the beauty of humility. Corporeal things have their ontological beauty, but this beauty is on a much lower plane and could not explain the sublimity of their beauty of form. This higher beauty of form in its quality transcends by far the sphere of these objects. The beauty of the Bay of Naples is of the highest spirituality and does not speak of that which mountains, trees, water signify ontologically, nor of that which they signify to a scientist or a philosopher of nature, but of a higher world which is reflected in it. It is a great mystery that God has entrusted to visible and audible objects, that they can place before us sublime, spiritual qualities: a beauty which, in its quality, reflects God's world, and which speaks of this higher transfigured world. The function of the senses and of the visible and audible contents in this is of a modest, humble kind: they are a pedestal, a mirror for something much higher. Therefore, this beauty in its rank is not bound to the ontological dignity of the object.

As a consequence, a flower is incomparably more beautiful than a worm, a Monte Pellegrino in Palermo, bathed in a sunset glow, is more beautiful than an animal, though the animal ranks higher ontologically. As soon as we understand that beauty of form (to be sure, adhering directly, intuitively, to the visible and audible and in no way resulting from reflections, analogies, or symbolic connections) cannot be attributed to the object in the same manner or does not speak of it, but is the ontological reflection of something incomparably higher, then we will also understand that it is absolutely false to designate it as sensuous, external, and particularly mundane. The beauty of the Italian landscape, of Tuscan villas, of Assisi, the beauty of the *Tempesta* by Giorgione, the frescoes of Masaccio in the Carmine, the beauty of Brunelleschi's cupola in Florence or of St. Peter's in Rome, or of Bach's *St. Matthew's Passion,* or of Mozart's *Figaro*—all this, to be sure, is immediately bound to audible and visible things; it is not related to beauty of form merely by thoughts; it is not ideas that these express thereby, but in their quality they speak about another, higher reality—they herald God.

The elements upon which beauty of form depends—i.e., when or under what circumstances it appears in visible and audible objects—are multiform and mysterious. There is no recipe, nor could anyone make rules to be followed to create something beautiful. Every individual case must have new, individual inspiration. One thing, however, we can determine: that the conditions be in the sphere of the visible and audible, like proportion, composition, melody, harmony, rhythm.

Here there is again revealed the whole mystery of the beauty of form, the transcendence in this sphere. Conditions that are apparently trifling and external have a strongly, profoundly, significantly spiritual effect. It depends on outward conditions, so to speak, whether a window opens, but what we see through the window when it is once open is weighty, significant, and by no means external. Again and again it is necessary to understand the mystery of this beauty of form. It directly adheres to visible and audible things, but the reality about which it speaks qualitatively, the being whose intrinsic fragrance it is, is a spiritual world towering high above everything corporeal. This is also brought out distinctly in the answer we give. The ontological beauty of a saint awakens in us a desire for closer communion with him, for we know that this beauty is a reflection of his personality.

With beauty of form, on the contrary, it is otherwise. The beauty of Monte Pellegrino in Palermo does not arouse the desire in us to caress it but, as we behold its beauty, our heart is filled with a desire for loftier regions about which this beauty speaks, and it looks upward with longing. In order to behold this beauty, we need not know God, much less think of Him; once we fully grasp this beauty it leads us to God, for objectively there is a reflection of Him in these things not merely in the manner in which all that exists reflects God. Here in things of a relatively low ontological rank something *appears* which surpasses by far their rank and heralds God in a more intimate way in its own quality. Only when we have understood this quasi-sacramental function of the visible and audible, this mystery that God has entrusted to it, can we do justice to the function of this beauty in the life of the redeemed. It is not true that this beauty distracts us from God and is specifically mundane. On the contrary, it contains a summons; in it there dwells a *sursum corda;* it awakens reverence in us; it elevates us above that which is base; it fills our hearts with a longing for the eternal beauty of God.

A misunderstanding also arises from the fact that all beauty is seen in the light of the beauty of the human face or body, and from the moral danger that can emanate from this conclusions are drawn about the "sensuality" of all beauty of form. Obviously these are false deductions. This beauty is accidentally connected with things that can appeal to sensuality. It is possible that here beauty of form can psychologically aggravate the kindling of concupiscence; in the case of the beauty of a landscape, a work of art, a symphony, it can no longer come into question. In general, to see beauty of form as an arousing of sensuality is nonsense. If anyone has a feeling for it, there resounds a sublime voice from above in the beauty of the adagio of Beethoven's Ninth Symphony; its quality speaks of a world of purity and spirituality; and he who hears it senses the incompatibility of all that is base and morally bad with this world. Yes, the exalted beauty of form is so far removed from drawing us down into the "world and its pomp" that there is a profound connection between this beauty and the realm of moral values. The breath of a higher world that dwells in beauty of form is also a *sursum corda* from the moral point of view.

Neither has all this been left behind and discarded by the Redemption. On the contrary, our relationship with all this beauty of form in nature and in art becomes something *different* and something new in Christ and through Christ, as does the relationship with all created values; it does not grow less, however, but becomes more profound and much greater.

Here we come upon a mysterious paradox: The more totally we give ourselves to God, the more we love God above all else, the deeper and truer is our love for all created things that really deserve our love. The inordinate attachment to earthly possessions, which can even degenerate into idolatry, is not a greater love, but a lesser, impurer, perverted one. The love of creatures, whether it be father, friend, or wife, can reach its full measure only in Christ, only by loving them in Christ and with Christ, indeed, only by partaking of the same love with which Christ loves them.

Thus the sense of this natural, qualitative message from God is not suppressed by the Redemption; it is set aright and transfigured by Christ. In all this beauty, which heralds God objectively, the redeemed will also consciously find God; he will trace this beauty back to its source; he will, indeed, seek and find in all the sublime beauty of the visible and audible world the countenance and the voice of the God-Man, Christ. The beauty of a landscape, of a great work of art is, thus, no less appreciated but, on the contrary, its comprehension is immeasurably more profound; it discloses *more* than it would to the eyes of the esthete who idolizes it with an inordinate love. All possessions that appeal to our pride and our concupiscence—indeed all that are merely subjectively satisfying—lose their radiance for the redeemed, for him who has found the pearl of great price of the Gospel. All possessions, however; that have real value, that are noble, precious, important in themselves, that fall like dew from above and ascend to God like incense, achieve a higher and new splendor in Christ. It is true that beauty of form does not belong to the *unum necessarium;* it is true that a person who has no feeling for it or who admires trash, can also become a saint and enter into heaven, just as one who is incapable of grasping philosophical truths and of distinguishing them from philosophical errors, who is intellectually limited and weak, could yet become a saint. But merely because something is not indispensable, it is not thereby prevented from possessing a profound and exalted value.

It is true that beauty of form does not belong to that which we must seek before all else. "Seek ye first the kingdom of God and His justice, and all these things shall be added unto you" (Luke 12:31) applies here also. This does not mean, however, that all else is without value. In this case, also, we should not say that the redeemed do not seek beauty of form before all else, but that they are first seeking the Kingdom of God, and in the same measure as they do so will they more and more appreciate this great gift of God and understand it. St. Francis of Assisi attests to this. How profoundly did he grasp the beauty of form in nature! How mysteriously did he, who sought only the Kingdom of God (I venture to say, *because* he sought the Kingdom of God), inspire the art and poetry of the thirteenth, fourteenth, and fifteenth centuries. And his spirit became the seed of one of the most important periods of florescence in art.

To the eyes of him who is redeemed, however, not only are deeper dimensions of the beauty of form revealed; he also understands clearly the significance of the beauty of form in his life. He understands, first of all, that God is glorified by things with beauty of form. He understands how greatly the world has been enriched by Mozart and Beethoven. He understands that the appearance of the house of God is not a matter of indifference, whether it be a fitting abode such as we find in the Cathedral of Chartres, in San Marco in Venice, where beauty speaks of God's world, or whether it exudes a desolate and depressing atmosphere like the false Gothic of the 'Eighties. He understands the claim that wherever anything makes Christ known, there nothing can be beautiful enough in the sense of beauty of form. He also understands the significance that beauty of form possesses as a spiritual nourishment even after the Redemption. It is not a matter of indifference whether a hymn to the Sacred Heart or to Our Lady be sentimental and trivial, or whether it be of a sublime and exalted beauty like the *Ave Verum* by Mozart, for triviality falsifies the world into which we are here to be drawn. Here the liturgy is again our great model. The liturgy of the Mass and of the Breviary, as the prayer of Christ, as an objectivation of the sacred life of the Church, clearly indicates in its construction, its form, its rhythm, and its Gregorian chant what role beauty of form plays in the light of Redemption, how it is also fit to speak to us of God, to lead us to God, to glorify God.

No one, perhaps, so clearly recognized the transcendence of the beauty of form and the fact that it is an efflorescence of a more exalted world than did the great Cardinal Newman, who also expressed it in these sublime words:

> There are seven notes in the scale; make them fourteen; yet what a slender outfit for so vast an enterprise! What science brings forth so much out of so little? Out of what poor elements does some great master in it create his new world? Shall we say that all this exuberant intensiveness is a mere ingenuity or trick of art like some game or fashion of the day without reality, without meaning? Or is it possible that that inexhaustible evolution and disposition of notes, so rich yet so simple, so intricate yet so regulated, so various yet so majestic, should be a mere sound which is gone and perishes? Can it be that those mysterious stirrings of the heart, and keen emotion, and strange yearnings after we know not what, and awful impressions from we know not whence, should be brought in us by what is unsubstantial, and comes and goes, and begins and ends in itself? It is not so; it cannot be. No; they have escaped from some higher sphere, they are the outpourings of eternal harmony in the medium of created sound; they are echoes of our home; they are the voice of angels, or the Magnificat of the Saints, or the Living Laws of Divine Governance, or Divine Attributes; something they are besides themselves, which we cannot encompass, which we cannot utter, though mortal man, and he perhaps not otherwise distinguished above his fellows, has the gift of eliciting them.[2]

[2] *University Sermons,* XV.

EFFICIENCY AND HOLINESS

"For where your treasure is, there will your heart be also."—*Luke* 12:34

MODERN anti-personalism instrumentalizes man and measures the importance and value of the individual person by his usefulness for some impersonal goods. It manifests itself not only in the idolatry of the state, the nation, the race, the class, but also in the overestimation of professional work and all kinds of efficiency. In our present epoch we are confronted with a "heresy of efficiency" which contradicts man's vocation and destiny and corrodes even the natural plenitude of a thoroughly human life.

The heresy of efficiency can be understood in three different ways, all of which are pertinent to our times. The first makes of man a mere means for the production of impersonal goods. It is revealed in every exploitation of men by a ruthless capitalism. Man is then considered to have no importance as a person, but only as an instrument for the production of other goods. This heresy culminates in the communist attitude toward man. As soon as man is no longer useful as an instrument, he is discarded as a worn-out tool.

The second type consists in an idolatry of man's great achievements in the field of art, of science, of technique, or even of films and sport. Thus efficiency in a higher sense of this term is here considered to be man's greatest value, his primary vocation. Man's center of gravity has been shifted from his moral center, from what he *is* as person to what he achieves.

The third type consists in an idolatry of work as such and especially of professional work.[1] It is a Calvinist and Puritan heritage identifying the serious part of life with work, and setting up an exclusive alternative of either work or amusement, relaxation and recreation.[2] Professional work and professional efficiency have become a kind of *causa exemplaris* for anything that is not pure recreation, amusement, or sport. The rhythm of professional work tends to become a *forma* of everything that is serious.

In this context it is impossible to enter into a detailed refutation of the first error. This error, ignoring the incomparable ontological superiority of man over impersonal creatures, is the very core of modern anti-personalism in all its different forms. It is the result of a progressive blindness concerning man's character as person, and it is a necessary consequence of the attempt to sever man from God.

As soon as we realize without prejudice the tremendous difference between a personal and an impersonal being, we cannot but grasp the incomparable ontological value of man as a person. Man alone is an image of God, while all impersonal beings are but traces of God. We must understand the new dimension of being in a person, who is a being possessing himself, endowed

[1] In stressing here the danger of an "idolatry" of work as such, we do not in any way intend to minimize the high moral role of work in man's life. Work, whatever its specific nature and purpose, has an important moral function for man's fallen nature. The danger of idleness has always been stressed. We have dealt with this aspect of work in *Transformation in Christ*, pp. 201–2.

[2] The words of Carlyle bespeak this mentality: "Work and do not despair."

with the capacity of knowledge and freedom of will, who is an awakened being, compared to which all impersonal beings "sleep," in order to understand that man's ontological value ranks higher than that of any impersonal being. Man can never be looked at as a means for impersonal goods. Man's soul is always incomparably more important than any impersonal good. This dignity of man versus anti-personalism is the great issue in the struggle that divides our present world into two camps. It is the lofty mission of our country to be the protagonist in the defense of this dignity and to protect it against its detractors.

We must dwell at greater length on the second error—the worship of great achievements and the primacy of achievement with respect to personality. The progressive process of secularization beginning in the Renaissance has, for many persons, destroyed the sense of the real end and destiny of man. In this mentality the center of gravity has been transferred from the being of the person as such to the sphere of achievement. And not only in judging other persons is this measure applied, but also in the evaluation of one's own person. One judges oneself to have worth to the extent that one is able to accomplish great things in one's profession. For this type of modern man, the ideal of efficiency has replaced the ideal of holiness.

The mentality of an epoch is characterized by those people who are the objects of its worship, those who, known by all, receive the greatest publicity. In the medieval epoch the name of a saint was on all lips, whereas in the Renaissance it was the name of a man of genius. Since then both have gradually been replaced by names of technicians and inventors. In the eighteenth century, the Pantheon in Paris was changed from a church dedicated to St. Genevieve to a monument for great men; i.e., men who were famous because of their achievements, such as social reformers, statesmen, scientists, artists, inventors. They seemed greater to this epoch than the saints to whom former times dedicated this church, and these "great men" seemed to call for worship more than Christ to whose divine sacrifice the church was built. Today the worship of great achievements has a tendency to degenerate into the worship of great businessmen, athletes, sportsmen, and movie actors.

Here we are confronted with the general fate of all idols. As soon as a created good is made an absolute and is deified, one progressively loses sight of its real value and this good deteriorates inevitably more and more.

The attempt to make man the absolute center of the universe has in reality led to a progressive blindness toward the true nature of his dignity. The attempt to make a god out of man ended in making of him a more highly developed ape. The idolatry of great achievements shares the same fate.

When confronting the worship of great achievements, it is imperative to recall man's primary vocation. Great as is the range of values which man is capable of realizing, moral values hold a unique position in man's life. They alone are indispensable for every human being, whatever his special gifts and talents may be.[3] They alone belong to the *unum necessarium*. Man is called above all to glorify God by his justice, his purity, his veracity, his goodness. "Be you perfect, as also your heavenly Father is perfect" (Matt. 5:48). Moral disvalues are an incomparable evil; they alone offend God; moral goodness reflects and glorifies God more than any achievement whatsoever.

But man is called to embody not only natural moral values: his real vocation is holiness, the *similitudo Dei*, the full unfolding of the divine principle of life received in Baptism. The primary vocation of man is transformation in Christ, which implies not only conformity with the natural moral law but embodiment of the incomparably higher supernatural virtues—i.e., holiness.

Compared with this vocation, the noblest talents, the creation of the greatest impersonal goods, are secondary. Progress in the domination of nature, inventions, great achievements in science, cultural activities, even the creation of master works in art—great as they are in themselves, much as they manifest man's greatness—do not constitute man's primary vocation. No excellence in these fields can be compared at all with the value embodied in a saint. Man's fitness for producing impersonal goods is not the cardinal question for him, but his virtues, his holiness, what he himself *is*, what personal values he realizes, and, above all, how

[3] Cf. D. von Hildebrand, *Christian Ethics*, chap. 15.

much Christ is reflected in him, how far he can say: "And I live, now not I, but Christ liveth in me." What ultimately counts is what a man is as a personality, and not what he has accomplished for science, for art, for culture, for politics, for technique, for economic affairs, for his country. The being of the person, i.e., his personality as such, is in the eyes of God more important than all impersonal goods that the person is able and called upon to bring forth.

In eternity man will not be judged according to his efficiency. It is high time to realize fully that the true reality which ultimately matters is not to be found in any far-reaching radius of action, not in any kind of efficacy, however great, which radiates to a large public. No, this full reality is to be found in personal values, above all, in the conformity of the human will to the divine will, in the free, unobstructed unfolding of the divine life in man—in his transformation in Christ.

Here it is essential to grasp a peculiar paradox: although the being of the person possesses an incontestable superiority over all "objective achievements," yet, on the other hand, it is proper to a person to be directed not toward himself, but toward objective values and to respond to them. It is in this very abandonment to objective values that the basic qualitative values of personal beings are constituted. These two apparently contradictory truths find a sublime mode of expression in certain passages taken from the Gospel. The sentence, "What doth it profit a man, if he gain the whole world, and suffer the loss of his own soul?" (Matt. 16:26) reveals clearly the primacy of the values embodied in the person over all the objective achievements he can bring about in the impersonal world. The words of Christ, "He that shall lose his life shall find it," clearly point to the fact that it belongs to the very essence of a personal being to abandon himself, indeed, to abandon himself to God.

Yet this self-abandonment does not mean primarily devotion to our professional work or to the production of apersonal goods. The moral values of the person constitute themselves rather in the free response to God and to all goods endowed with a morally relevant value. In obedience to the commandments of Christ, in the love of God and the love of neighbor, in the loving imitation of Christ alone, can man be transformed into Christ and fulfill his primary vocation. This abandonment alone is the way to holiness.

At this point it is necessary to distinguish between three main categories of professional work.

The first category embraces all professions whose end is either an indispensable good or a useful one, such as the work of a carpenter, a shoemaker, or a factory worker. This category also embraces professions whose end is the production of merely subjectively satisfying goods such as candies, liquors, toys. Most professions belong to this first category, as well as workers, artisans, most employees, secretaries, clerks, and office workers.

The second category embraces professions concerned with goods endowed with a high intrinsic value. To this category belongs the work of artists, poets, musicians, philosophers, scientists, statesmen, physicians, teachers, educators.

Whereas the first category of work possesses its dignity and seriousness insofar as it is work, or because of the usefulness of its purpose, the second category derives dignity and seriousness primarily from the high values of the goods in question.

The third category of professions is in reality no longer a mere profession, but rather a special *vocation*. We have in mind the "profession" of the priest, of the missionary, of the bishop whose activity is in the vineyard of the Lord.

Now, every profession has also a specifically human element: for instance, the attitude of the businessman toward his clients and employees, the attitude of the journalist toward truth, the attitude of the worker toward his co-workers and his manager. This element of the profession, due to the fact that it concerns our relation to other persons, is obviously relevant to the attainment of holiness. But every profession has also an element determined exclusively by its specific aim. The perfect performance of a profession can also be judged by the immanent laws of its end. We call a businessman proficient, for instance, when he knows how to make money, i.e., how to make his respective business flourish. We speak of a doctor as good when we acknowledge his diagnoses as correct and admit that he knows how to cure an illness. Desirable as it is for a man to be proficient in his work, we must understand that his being a great poet, an outstanding inventor, an excellent engineer, or a brilliant scientist in no way fulfills the vocation to which Christ calls him when He says: "Follow Me."

Even when we prescind from the human element of professional work, it requires for its perfection not only skill, talent, and intelligence, but also certain moral qualities. Assiduity, punctuality, reliability, a spirit of responsibility are all indispensable requirements for any degree of efficiency. The degree of efficiency expressly depends upon the degree to which these qualities are present, and a complete lack of these qualities would frustrate any professional activity.

Whereas these moral presuppositions are common to all kinds of work and belong to the very nature of efficiency in general, the attainment of the end implies other and higher moral qualities for professions belonging to the second category mentioned above. In order, for instance, to be a great artist or a great philosopher, special moral qualities are required.

In order to be great, an artist must have an artistic conscience. Neither the desire of making more money nor the ambition of being more popular, nor any other motive, should lead him to betray the dictates of true artistic beauty. He must, in fact, have an incorruptible devotion to artistic beauty. He must likewise always preserve the awareness that he is responsible for developing the talents entrusted to him. In order to be great, a philosopher must have an incorruptible desire for truth, the humility to admit his own limitations, the readiness to abandon what he has constructed the instant reality requires it, and that reverence which enables him to listen to the voice of being.

In these cases, then, high moral values are required for the intrinsic perfection of professional work. There is, however, another connection between moral virtues and the immanent perfection of professional work; namely, in those cases in which the profession has the character of a direct service rendered to other human beings. The professions of teaching and nursing, for example, have in their very performance a specifically human and morally relevant character. Charity and patience on the part of an educator are among the foremost presuppositions for a successful and good education.[4] Apart from the intelligence and the capacity for

[4] It could possibly be objected that in every profession a spirit of sacrifice and unselfish devotion increases the immanent perfection of the work. A secretary who is exceedingly diligent—always ready to work overtime, a clerk who is so dedicated to his task that he shuns no burden nor sacrifice connected with his job, are both undoubtedly more efficient and more perfect from the point of view of a merely immanent perfection of the work. Yet these moral qualities function here more as means of increasing the usefulness of the worker, and do not refer to the intrinsic quality of the work itself. Moreover, the devotion and sacrifice of the secretary or the clerk have a real moral value only if either the good with which the work is concerned justifies this devotion because of its high value; or if the employer for whom they work is so needy that the efforts exhibited are an outgrowth of charity. If, on the contrary, this devotion and this spirit of sacrifice are mere manifestations of temperament, or a "being absorbed" by the immanent law of working, or an exaggeration of the importance of work, or even an escape into work, this devotion and spirit of sacrifice have no longer a real moral value. It is unnecessary to say that all efforts due to selfish interest have no moral value whatsoever. The capitalist who allows himself no intermission in his work and chooses the life of an ascetic in order to make his business more flourishing manifests anything but moral virtue. Summarizing, we can say that so long as no good endowed with high values is at stake, efficiency includes only these more formal moral virtues of assiduity, punctuality, and so on, which we mentioned above.

understanding the child's soul, charity and patience, as well as firmness and justice are indispensable for the good educator. In the field of nursing also we must note that in addition to the requirements of medical training, intelligence, skill, and competence, the constant exercise of charity and patience, an indefatigable spirit of sacrifice and an ever-present meekness and firmness are essential requisites for the good nurse.[5] In an analogous way, though not to the same extent, certain moral virtues belong to the immanent perfection of the doctor. As concerns the third category, i.e., work in the vineyard of the Lord, it must be said that these activities are indeed such that in order to fulfill them perfectly nothing short of holiness is necessary. In the frame of these sacred activities there is no place for mere efficiency, not even in the highest sense of this term.

It is obvious that perfection in the first category of professions and the greatest efficiency in professional work in no way imply the fulfillment of man's primary vocation. First, the moral requirements for any kind of efficiency, such as assiduity, punctuality, or a spirit of responsibility, in no way guarantee the presence of higher moral values, e.g., justice, veracity, and above all the fruits of the Holy Ghost, such as humility and charity. Second, these moral requirements alone still do

[5] Unfortunately, today, the essential role of these moral values requisite in a good nurse are too frequently overlooked, and consequently the erroneous belief has arisen that mere knowledge and scientific training suffice. The fact is that a nurse with the best possible training and the greatest skill is not a good nurse, even from the point of view of merely immanent perfection, if she does not possess these moral qualities.

not guarantee professional perfection. Thus one can become a saint even though thoroughly inefficient in one's profession. The disciple of St. Francis of Assisi, the blessed Brother Juniper, was a saint despite the fact that he was a very bad cook.

Concerning even the second category of professions in which the end is a good having a high value—for instance, in the case of an artist, of a philosopher, or of a statesman—the professional perfection as such in no way implies the fulfillment of man's primary vocation. Although for perfect achievement these professions presuppose, as we saw, moral qualities apart from the general moral requirements of efficiency, the possession of these moral qualities is still far from being equivalent to holiness. Thus, even in this second category, it is not by virtue of their professional perfection that men can become saints. If a saint happened to be great in his profession, he was a saint not because of this fact, but because of the fact that aside from his professional perfection *he loved God above all and his neighbor as himself*. St. Augustine, St. Thomas Aquinas, St. Bonaventure were saints, not because they were great philosophers, but because they were endowed with heroic virtues. St. Jeanne d'Arc has been canonized, not because she was a great and successful general, but because she was transformed in Christ.

And even with reference to these sacred professions which are perhaps more aptly called special vocations, their perfection is not merely identical with the fulfillment of man's primary vocation. Though it may be said here that holiness is an indispensable presupposition for the perfect fulfillment of the special vocation, and that thus the ideal Pope is necessarily a saint, it may happen that holiness does not always guarantee the perfect fulfillment of these special vocations. St. Peter Celestine was not a competent Pope. He resigned voluntarily. Dante placed him in Hell in his *Divina Commedia,* but the Church canonized him.

The exaggerated importance placed on the role of professional work can be traced to another error of a more general nature: the overstressing of the more or less specialized task that each person has by reason of his particular talent, by virtue of his position in the world. It may be said that we have a tendency today to overemphasize differences. We underscore, for example, the diversity of religious orders and the particular form characteristic of each; we compare the piety of one epoch with that of other epochs; we stress the individual note of each saint. And in so doing we tend to lose sight of that which is common to *all* religious orders, to the true piety of *all* epochs, and, above all, to that which is essentially common to all saints. In the same way we exaggerate the differences between the tasks imposed by the possession of various talents. We slip into the danger of thinking that the task of each individual person consists *primarily* in discharging one particular function in the whole. We underline the factors that distinguish the tasks proper to men from those proper to women. And all the time we tend to overlook the one great task which underlies and rises superior to every specialization, which is the primary call of every person as person: that is, personal sanctification, which means being transformed in Christ and radiating Him. And this radiation in its most central point is not specified by the particular place each person occupies in the cosmos.

The great French philosopher Gabriel Marcel has indicated the danger of instrumentalization and depersonalization of man in this ominous passage:

> Travelling on the Underground, I often wonder with a kind of dread what can be the inward reality of the life of this or that man employed on the railway—the man who opens the doors, for instance, or the one who punches the tickets. Surely everything both within him and outside him conspires to identify this man with his functions as worker, as trade union member or as voter, but with his vital functions as well. The rather horrible expression "time table" perfectly describes his life. So many hours for each function. Sleep too is a function which must be discharged so that the other functions may be exercised in their turn. The same with pleasure, with relaxation; it is logical that the weekly allowance of recreation is a psycho-organic function which must not be neglected any more than, for instance, the function of sex. We need go no further; this sketch is sufficient to suggest the emergence of a kind of vital schedule; the details will vary with the country, the climate, the profession, etc., but what matters is that there is a schedule.
>
> It is true that certain disorderly elements—sickness, accidents of every sort—will break in on the smooth working of the system. It is therefore natural that the individual should be overhauled at regular intervals

like a watch (this is often done in America). The hospital plays the part of the inspection bench or the repair shop. And it is from this same standpoint of function that such essential problems as birth control will be examined.

As for death, it becomes, objectively and functionally, the scrapping of what has ceased to be of use and must be written off as total loss.[6]

To lose sight of the primary vocation of man, as does this heresy of efficiency, has disastrous social consequences. When a man judges himself to be worth only as much as his performance is worth, social disparities necessarily become unbridgeable abysses.[7] The difference between a statesman or an artist or a factory worker who performs only one and the same movement all day long is obviously enormous, and if the workman judges himself in terms of the value of his profession, he must feel himself to be a pariah, condemned by an unjust fate.

This remains true even if the worker is told that his labor is indispensable and that it receives its importance and impact through the service rendered by it to the community. Although it is true that this gives to

[6] *The Philosophy of Existence,* trans. Manya Harari (London, 1948), p. 2. Quoted with permission of the publisher, the Harvill Press. Cf. also Marcel's *The Mystery of Being* (Chicago, 1950), I, chap. 2, "A Broken World."

[7] It is true that every worker, especially in the United States, may hope to work himself up and attain an influential and important position. But this hope is a vague one and will be realized in very few cases only. Moreover, this improvement, apart from the replacement of manual work by a work of organization, has more bearing upon the financial situation of the person in question than upon the gratifying and interesting character of the work.

every work an indirect significance above the immediate activity, this significance alone is not enough to bridge the abyss that separates the work of a scientist from that of a shoeshine.

It may be further objected that every work can be done better or worse. To accomplish a work in a perfect manner is a source of satisfaction independent of the special content of the work. Thus, even the man whose professional work is such that in comparing his labor with that of others it cannot but give him a consciousness of inferiority, finds a source of self-assertion in the formal perfection in which the work is accomplished. But if it is true that this formal efficiency may be a source of satisfaction, it does not suffice to span the abyss separating the different categories of profession.

If, on the contrary, he feels himself to be worth as much as he is as a person, according to his relation to God and his neighbor, and his responses to all authentic values, if he grasps the common vocation of all men and the common and main sources of happiness, the differences between the respective professions vanish and can no longer constitute insurmountable walls between the different classes.

Closely linked to the shifting of our center of gravity from the personality into achievements is the third type of heresy of efficiency, which sees in work the prototype of seriousness and which finds its expression in the disastrous alternative: either work or amusement.

This alternative leaves no place for man's direct converse with God, which manifests itself in prayer, religious contemplation, the I-thou love relation to Christ. It moreover entails the destruction of all natural plenitude and the depth of a thoroughly human life. Amusement insofar as it is morally unobjectionable is certainly something legitimate. Only an austere Jansenistic view could consider it an evil as such. But as soon as we approach goods endowed with a high value as if they were in the category of amusement, the understanding for their depth and dignity—as well as any adequate response to them—is frustrated.

Relaxation and recreation are not only legitimate as amusement, but are even a necessary and indispensable element in man's life. Only gnostic exaltation could deny the necessity of giving a place to recreation, which is obligatory even in the most severe monasteries. Yet necessary as moments of recreation and relaxation are in human life, it is fatal for the depth of life the moment they became the "title" for all things apart from professional work.

As soon as anything is approached as if it were recreation or relaxation or even as if it were amusement, a register is drawn which bars every deep experience. The register which is precisely indispensable in order to relax, and which is the appropriate approach for games, movies, and certain types of sport, implies a certain "periphery" and above all the absence of an inner *élan.* In saying periphery we do not mean that while relaxing we should be cut off from our depth, that we should give up the *habitare secum* and fall away from the basic attitude of *religio*. Such "letting ourselves go" is never legitimate. Yet relaxation implies that even though we superactually remain in contact with our deeper stratum, we put off spiritual *élan* and recollection. It is analogous to sleep. In order to fall asleep, we must accomplish this inner relaxation, and in case we find it difficult to fall asleep we try to place ourselves in this state of inner relaxation.

In turning to recreation and relaxation, we turn to the periphery, we let ourselves be distracted; and we give rest to the organs in the depths of our soul—those organs whose very function is to "concert" with great and important things. Thus it is impossible to do justice to goods endowed with high values, as soon as we approach them in a mood of relaxation or recreation. To approach them as something destined for the time of recreation and relaxation, or even as mere amusement, is equivalent to a frustration of any real communion with them.

The disastrous alternative which sets up work on the one hand as the serious part of life and amusement and relaxation on the other as the non-serious part completely ignores the existence of another antithesis to work, which consists in the emergence from the specific tension and concentration of work to a recollection, i.e., a *contemplative* turning to God and to goods endowed with high values. We must not confuse relaxation in which we enter into the periphery with the essentially different "relaxation" in which we reach a depth superior to that of work.

The *vacare* of which St. Augustine speaks as an element of beatitude when in *The City of God* he says "*Vacabimus et videbimus,*" implies the absence of the tension and preoccupation typical of professional work. It certainly differs still more from the peripherical relaxation of recreation.

The intellectual intuition of metaphysical truth, the fruition of sublime beauty, and the adoration of God are specifically contemplative attitudes. And these contemplative attitudes clearly imply a specific depth, which is the actualization of the deepest stratum of our soul. The superior depth of contemplative attitudes is also manifested in the fact that they require a good endowed with high values as their object. Merely neutral and indifferent things such as a machine or mechanical processes themselves cannot as such become objects of our contemplation. Only when an object has something deep and essential to communicate can it become the object of a contemplative attitude. Only an object endowed with high values, i.e., only an object reflecting God in such a way that it is capable of leading us *in conspectu Dei,* is truly capable of being an object of contemplation. The virtues of a person, an important and deep truth, or a sublime beauty in nature or art, are such possible objects for contemplation—are worthy to be contemplated. As well, the higher the object ranks, the more sublime is its value, the more intimately does it reflect God, the more imperatively does it call for a contemplative response. In opening our souls to the radiation of Christ, and in the loving adoration of Christ, alone do we attain that supreme contemplative attitude which is the actualization of our ultimate depth. To the extent that the modern world has lost faith, the ideals of work and achievement have replaced religion.

For the modern mind, morality, embracing the luminous world of supernatural and natural virtues, is largely restricted to those moral values that are requisite for efficiency in professional work. The interest no longer centers on humility, purity, charity, holy patience, meekness, and justice, but revolves instead around reliability, honesty, assiduity, self-control, and politeness. Efficiency has replaced virtue.

Morality is legalized and seen in the light of efficiency. It is increasingly deprived of the victorious quality of moral goodness with its intrinsic beauty, and, as a result, assumes an aspect of mere correctness. The fundamental difference between a positive law of state and a moral commandment is no longer clearly grasped.

The substitution of efficiency for virtue manifests itself particularly in the fact that morality is no longer comprised of the moral obligations concerning the human part of our professional life but is, instead, reduced to the virtues presupposed for the fulfillment of the end of the profession as such. We saw before that every profession implies certain human elements: the contact of the worker with his associates and his superiors, the contact of the doctor with his patients and his colleagues are such examples. These human elements specifically imply a number of moral obligations and also provide numerous instances for the development of morally good or evil attitudes, such as patience, charity, veracity, justice, or their opposites. Yet an atheist would not tend to equate morality with the realm of these virtues in professional life, but rather with such attitudes as reliability, honesty, punctuality, assiduity in the fulfillment of the professional work as such, co-operativeness, team spirit. Morality is neutralized, and duty has lost its moral impact.

Today there exists not only an idolatry of work and efficiency, but also a hypertrophy of amusement. The present deification of work does not imply that one's entire life should be filled with work, or that men work more today than they did in former epochs. There is, on the contrary, a strong tendency to restrict the time of work. Amusement and entertainment play a tremendous role and are considered an essential part of life. Indeed, a man is deemed frustrated if amusement is not accessible to him.

We previously noted that the whole approach to the human element of life is in terms of amusement or relaxation. All great and deep human things, however, are not only desubstantialized and falsified by this approach, but they are also replaced more and more by amusement in the literal sense. Movies, television, baseball, the comics—all increasingly fill the time meant for deep or intimate conversation with those we love, the time needed for contemplation of beauty in nature and art, or that time intended for the reading of good books.[8]

Family and conjugal life must necessarily become denuded of its soul when it is classed in the category of amusement or recreation. It is true that many workers may come home exhausted by their work, worn out, desirous only of relaxing. But the exhaustion through work is not the main reason for the wrong approach to family and conjugal life. Even the restriction of the day's work, legitimate as it is in itself, does not change anything basic while the general attitude remains which considers work as the only serious part of life. Leisure time will be spent in going to movies and in frequenting bars. How will marriage keep its intrinsic dignity if conjugal life, instead of being considered something deep and serious, and as the moment of recollected leisure, is viewed as the time intended for "taking it easy" and for relaxing? [9]

Deeply characteristic of this perversion of our times is the fact that the holy day of Sunday, the day of con-

[8] The modern alternative of work on the one hand and amusement on the other is, in a certain way, an expression of infantilism. It is normal for children to consider school as being the serious part of life and to identify seriousness with unpleasant, burdensome tasks. The child is free to play only when schoolwork is done, and playing thus becomes more or less identified with the joyful.

[9] This same unfortunate alternative has sometimes grave consequences in education. Many guilt complexes are due to the fact that work is considered to be the only serious part of life. Some people feel morally guilty as soon as they are not working. They even feel "guilty" when they give their time to some important human affair rather than to professional work, even though in doing so they behave in the morally right way.

templation and recollection, the first day of the week, and its most important day, the day which gives to the entire week its *forma* and meaning, and which could be called the *antiphon* of the entire week, has been replaced by the week end, meant only for amusement and relaxation.

The disastrous alternative of work or amusement is not without influence even on those who still have faith. These people certainly do not replace religion with work, but nevertheless they too frequently see religious life in the light of work. The fact that professional work has become the prototype of seriousness has created a tendency to fulfill one's religious duties in a spirit analogous to that used in working. In leaving no place for the contemplative attitude, prayers, even the contemplative mental prayer, are made a "work," performed in an attitude of dutiful efficiency. A spirit of loyalty, order, regularity, and punctuality, precisely taken from the realm of professional work or from the ethos of a functionary, replaces the genuine religious mentality, which is always pervaded by a spirit of contemplation, and which always implies an ascent to a completely different supernatural reality, i.e., a dwelling before the ineffably holy God. When professional work because of its usefulness, its sober activity, and its concentration on the immanent logic of a being and an activity becomes the pattern of seriousness, religious life is necessarily secularized and deprived of its sacred breath and of its *sursum corda*. The danger of exaggerating the importance of professional work is such that sometimes even the work in the vineyard of the

Lord is viewed in the light of professional work. The tendency arises to approach it as if it were a "job" and consequently one can too easily slip into the erroneous belief that assiduity, punctuality, reliability, and efficiency are the foremost requirements for fulfilling this vocation.

Instead of understanding that these activities which are directly concerned with the Kingdom of Heaven are something incomparably more sublime than and totally different from any profession, many persons incline to secularize them in that they regard them as merely professional activities. The opinion is sometimes expressed that there is no essential difference because every profession, whatever it may be, is a service of God if only it is accomplished in the right spirit and with the right intention. It is true that every work can be sanctified by the right intention; it requires, however, that instead of seeing the direct service of God in the light of a job, all professional work be formed by the primary vocation of all men: our sanctification.

This is an error analogous to the one made in asking why one should spend so much time in praying when one's work also is prayer if accomplished with the right intention.

Again, we must concede that indeed all work can and should become a prayer in an analogous sense. But this is possible only when we clearly distinguish between authentic prayer—i.e., prayer in praise, in thanks, or in petition, or mental prayer—and all forms of work. It is only when this authentic prayer, in which we are directed to God and focused on God in a contemplative rhythm, holds an important place in our life, that it will be able to stamp all our activities with its style and ethos.[10]

The specifically human part of life is often approached by Catholics as being composed, on the one hand, of moral duties, on the other hand of amusement, recreation, and relaxation. The moral part of marriage and the moral part of friendship are approached as something serious, but the fruition of a deep conversation with beloved persons, the common experience of high spiritual goods, are approached as belonging to the part of life designated as recreation, relaxation, or amusement. The deep experience of beauty in nature and art is "taken seriously," if it is necessary for our professional work, if we need it for our studies, or in order to fulfill our duties as teacher. But in itself this noble fecundation of our soul by beauty, this gift of God's bounty, this message of His glory and of a higher world above us, is treated as if it belonged to recreation or relaxation, and as if it were permissible under this title only. Sometimes it may even be approached merely as amusement.

Yet all the great human sectors of life—our relations to beloved persons, a deep and holy conversation, the impact of the message of God in the beauty of nature, the contemplation of a great truth—they all are deprived of their depth and meaning as soon as they are approached as mere amusement and recreation. If instead of putting on festival garments, when we turn to

[10] Cf. Josef Pieper, *Leisure, the Basis of Culture,* trans. Alexander Dru (New York, 1952).

the specifically human part of our life, we even cease to be on our best behavior and to pull ourselves together as we do in our professional work, and simply relax, we cut ourselves off from the real meaning and content of these high goods and frustrate our genuine human life.

Professional work itself must be integrally incorporated in our vocation, and must become a way of manifesting this primary vocation.

The first requirement for an organic incorporation of professional work into our vocation is the full awareness of the primacy of man's vocation to be transformed into Christ, with respect to his profession, whatever it may be. This awareness implies above all that we avoid falling prey to the immanent logic of an activity. Although we should attempt to be at our best in every professional activity, and although this is possible only if we conform to its immanent logic, we must never be absorbed by the immanent logic; we must not be drawn into a whirlpool of activity—i.e., into the automatic rhythm of work as such. While performing any professional activity, we must never forget the words of our Lord: "Martha, Martha, thou art careful, and art troubled about many things; but one thing is necessary. Mary hath chosen the best part."

We must from time to time emerge from work and turn for a moment to Christ, dwell before God, recollect ourselves. This alone can make any professional work a manifestation of our primary vocation and grant to it the character of an apostolate. Only if contemplation has its place in the life of man will this danger of absorption by the immanent logic of professional work be immunized.

Work in the frame of the first category of professional work should never arrogate to itself the same place in the life of man which work of the second category may fill and still less that which work in the third category should fill.

It would be a typical symptom of the heresy of efficiency to deal with professions of the first category after the pattern of professions belonging to the second category. Professional work of the first category is primarily a means to earn money which should be used for indispensable things and things possessing a value. In most cases this professional work is a means of earning our living and that of our dependents. It is completely legitimate for a worker to approach his work primarily as a means for making money. For the professions of the second category, on the contrary, the primary motive must never be to make money. An artist who considers his work primarily as a means of earning money desecrates his mission and is in great danger of acting against his artistic conscience by using cheap and trite effects. Analogously it is definitely illegitimate for a philosopher or a scientist to look at his work primarily as a means for a more comfortable life; like the artist, he has to be a servant of his work. A doctor of medicine who approaches his work primarily as a source of making money acts immorally and contradicts the dignity of the work entrusted to him. This fact clearly illustrates the difference in the approach to professional work in the two categories.

In order to incorporate the professional work of the first category in our primary vocation, it definitely has to play a secondary role with respect to the *human* part of our life. It must not be the source from which the value and meaning of our life derive, even from a purely natural point of view, nor be the main source of our happiness.

We have to keep a certain distance from it and never forget its character of *means,* if we are to avoid the heresy of efficiency. This does not mean, however, that the ideal approach to this type of work would be to consider it as a mere inevitable means which has nothing to offer us besides the money we earn through it. On the contrary, the proficient performance of a work and the consciousness of doing something useful or even indispensable are both sources of legitimate satisfaction.[11]

In this respect there are again great differences to be found in the frame of the first category of professions. The work of artisans offers a source of joy which differs from that of factory workers. The progress of technique and the overwhelming role of the machine in man's professional activities have, on the one hand, eased work, and increased the possibility of attaining the end more quickly and sometimes more accurately, but, on the other hand, they have denuded man's work of its soul and its organic character. We clearly see this in compar-

[11] It is true that the satisfaction of mastering something is experienced in games in which we are champions; when professional work is in question, however, the gratification deriving from a perfect accomplishment assumes another quality and a more serious character.

ing the work of an artisan with the production of the same article in a factory. The creative, organic process of working and the direct relation to its product give to the artisan's work a human character. The factory worker who repeats one isolated activity, who is no longer in direct contact with the finished product, has become a servant of the machine, a means in the production of those goods. The artisan, on the contrary, is not a servant, but the master in the process of production.

In the work of some artisans there is also an element of creative shaping and molding which is a kind of prelude to artistic activity. This is above all the case in all those activities of artisans which are connected with applied art. The products of the work have definitely a charm and aesthetic value, and this work possesses an outspoken human personal character. It is radically opposed to mechanical work on a machine in a factory. The work of this artisan has a classic character and a dignity of its own. The immanent task of the artisan thus has, apart from the usefulness of its product, the capacity to puzzle and interest him, to challenge his talents and his skill. The artisan should aim not only at the perfection of the good he produces, because of a sense of duty, but he should also take interest in it for its own sake and rejoice when he succeeds in making it well.[12] Thus an artisan loves his work; he may be attached to it for its own sake, independently of its usefulness to him.

[12] Cf. Adolf von Hildebrand, *Arbeiter und Arbeit,* Gesammelte Aufsätze (Strasburg, 1916).

In a quite different way the farmer's work (especially if it is not mechanized through machines) also has a classic human character and a dignity. Here it is the co-operation with nature's generosity, the concerting with life which opposes this activity to all mechanical activities in which man is instrumentalized. The farmer, therefore, may also find a source of joy in his work.

A factory worker doing a mechanical and monotonous work cannot find the same source of joy in his work, but here the feeling of co-operation in the production of useful or even indispensable goods can also give the work a meaning apart from its money-earning function.

Yet, despite the fact that the different types of work should have a meaning beyond being a source of income—some because of the objective task implied in the work, some because of the usefulness of the goods to whose production the work pertains in whatever modest way—it remains true that this type of work should always be secondary in rank, with respect to the human part of life.

This type of work will be incorporated in man's primary vocation if it remains subordinate to the human part of life, and if in the frame of the profession itself its human part is stressed more than the mere immanent perfection of the work.

But this again will be possible only to the extent that contemplation and contemplative attitudes have their place in our life. Professional work of the first category, since it never requires the depth of "engagement" indispensable for the professional work of the second category, makes it easier to remain superactually united with Christ while doing the work.

But the immanent perfection even of this work will be increased by contemplation. It is only in this contemplative recollection that man becomes able to mobilize a full "engagement." [13]

Apart from all the factors of talent, disposition, skill, experience, training which determine the quality of the professional work in this first category, the question of how much a person commits himself plays a great role. The degree of our readiness to commit ourselves is a moral question; and we are able to actualize this moral "engagement" and perseverance only if our life is embedded in a contemplative rhythm.

It is of the utmost importance to understand that this "engagement" which we observe in the lives of the saints, even in the most modest professional work, must not only be clearly distinguished from sheer absorption in the work but is even incompatible with falling prey to its immanent logic.

Great efficiency may readily be combined with an absorption by the immanent logic of professional work

[13] By the expression "full engagement" we do not mean a complete engagement involving deeper strata of our soul, which is required only for professional work of the second category. We mean the full, conscious pledge that the work in question requires in order to be performed perfectly, the full investment of our energy and attention as opposed to any perfunctory manner of performance.

and the heresy of overrating it; the type of "engagement" we are aiming at is incompatible with this absorption. And above all the Christian ethos of this kind of profession implies, on the one hand, the inner freedom, the readiness to yield as soon as a higher good calls for it, and, on the other, this full "engagement." Both derive from the same abandonment to Christ, from the awareness that "we belong to Christ."

So far as the second category of professional work is concerned, the role of contemplation offers a new aspect. Besides the above-mentioned general indispensability of contemplation for the incorporation of any profession into our primary vocation, professions of this second type presuppose a spirit of contemplation in order to be perfect. In fact, the importance of contemplation for the immanent perfection of a professional work increases in proportion to the rank of the good with which a profession deals.[14] The work of an artist, a philosopher, an educator, requires a contemplative basis as the indispensable presupposition for the depth and inner plenitude of any activity involving a good

[14] We must emphasize that the primary importance of contemplation does not lie in the influence it has on the quality of professional work, but in itself. In mentioning that this "engagement" which enhances efficiency is possible only on the basis of a confrontation with Christ, we do not intend to construe this confrontation as a means to efficiency. Our topic here is the *incorporation* of professional work into our primary vocation; as we saw before, it is not at all the degree of efficiency that is the norm. But it is important to see that this incorporation, far from excluding professional efficiency, alone can inform our work with this "engagement" without imprisoning us in its immanent rhythm. Here, as everywhere, we find confirmation of the words of Our Lord: "Seek ye first the kingdom of God and His justice. . . ."

endowed with high values. We have to receive in order to be able to give. Our soul has to be fecundated in order to give birth to great and important things.

Now, it is precisely the contemplative attitude, freed from the tension of activity, possessing this de-pragmatized openness, which is the presupposition for a fecundation of our soul, for attaining the inner wealth indispensable for every creative activity. It is a well-known experience that a whirlpool of activity in which we run from one immediate goal to another, in which we never come to ourselves, empties us and deprives any deeper activity of its inner plenitude. We feel empty and dull when we do not have renewed moments of recollection and contemplation. Thus we see that insofar as it is a question of professions which by their very content and rank call for a greater role in our life than those of the first category, contemplation plays a specific role for the very perfection of professional achievement. If, in general, these professions do not allow us the same opportunity for being concerned with the human part of our profession and apostolate, apart from the professional work, but by their very nature call for a deeper engagement of our person, nevertheless they provide another kind of opportunity because they are themselves related to our primary vocation. And this also finds its expression in the indispensable role of contemplation for the very quality of this work.

Yet when we turn to the third category of profession, the role of contemplation is an incomparably greater one. For the work in the vineyard of the Lord, contemplation is so necessary that without it the greatest activity, supported by the most brilliant natural talents, would remain as a sounding brass or a tinkling cymbal.

Here the words of St. Bernard apply, when he says that our soul should not be like a channel through which grace runs, but like a fountain that overflows. If it is to bear fruit, the work in the vineyard of the Lord has to be Christ's work through us, and this is possible only if we let our soul be fecundated time and again by Christ, by dwelling in a contemplative attitude before Him, by listening to Christ as St. Mary Magdalen listened, by exposing our souls in silence and recollection to His irradiation.

Second, each profession can be conceived as an opportunity for a personal apostolate to the extent that it includes or brings about contacts with other persons. Almost every profession offers many situations in which one can radiate Christ through one's being, in which one can act as apostle. It is not the specific content of one's profession which is to be considered here as medium for one's primary vocation, but rather the opportunity of contact with other men which one's profession may present. One's profession is here conceived as an opportunity for the apostolate and for the extension of God's kingdom. This opportunity is granted in professions that are poor in content, such as that of the factory worker, as well as in professions rich in content, such as that of the artist. This possibility of apostolate increases in proportion as one's profession includes a wider contact with other persons, and as the human part, mentioned above, plays a greater role.

It is true that the immanent perfection of profes-

able. The fact that, desirous to provide for the necessities of life, an employee accepts a given work entitles him to consider this work as the place assigned to him by Providence, and thus he can and should also feel himself as God's steward, when he is doing his work well.

It does not, however, apply to those employers who neither produce nor distribute goods that are indispensable or really useful, nor who must work in order to earn a living, but who want only to make money for the sake of money or in order to be able to satisfy their every wish in the frame of things attained by money. Though it is certainly not immoral to try to amass a fortune just in order to be wealthy, it is not possible to feel oneself as God's steward in this type of work. If money is heaped up with the intention of serving goods endowed with a high value, such as religious, cultural, or social purposes, or in order to help individual persons in need, or with the intention of making their lives easier and more joyful, then, obviously, such work has again an inner significance which entitles the employer to feel that he is God's steward.

This consecration of one's profession is much more than a mere good intention. During the whole performance of our professional activity we must remain conscious of the fact that we do not belong to ourselves but to Christ, and that we must remain superactually united to Him.

Fourth, one's profession can and should be incorporated in one's vocation as a Christian in such a manner that it is conceived as a service to God, on the basis of the immanent relationship existing between its content and the Kingdom of God.

This is not possible in the first category of professions. In the second category, however, because of the intrinsic connection the purpose of the profession has with the Kingdom of God, the immanent perfection of these professions can rightly be conceived as a special service of God. But in the third category the immanent perfection is even indissolubly linked with this intention and approach.

Here it should be stressed emphatically that it is a senseless undertaking to try to establish this fourth type of incorporation with every profession in a like manner. One should humbly acknowledge that there is an objective hierarchy of professions, and not try to draw out of a profession what is simply not in it.

The attempt to level all professions is a logical consequence of the overestimation of professional work, and of the fact that the consciousness of one's vocation to holiness and to the apostolate of Christ is not fully alive. One wants to bring about a compensation within the frame of professions, instead of seeing that workers as well as kings, artisans as well as artists, research men as well as merchants, are not primarily workers, kings, or the like, but members of the Mystical Body of Christ, persons who have received Christ and who are called to become holy, to reflect Christ.

In the degree to which a profession is unimportant in its substance, this fourth form of incorporation must recede to the background in favor of the three other forms of incorporation. A street-cleaner can certainly not lay claim to being filled by his work and molded through his work in the manner that an artist or a scientist can. But the very fact that a humble work does not fill and mold one as does a higher profession gives to him who performs it the opportunity to turn directly to God, a relationship that cannot be established through the content of the work alone.

Finally, one's profession can be integrated with one's vocation by performing it as a service to the community. In each profession there is a relationship to the community, and it is therefore possible to consider it as an efflux of love for one's neighbor.

In performing a work in the spirit of the words: "As long as you did it for one of these, the least of my brethren, you did it for me," every profession, however poor in content, will receive significance and be incorporated in man's primary vocation.

Not until this absolute primacy of one's vocation as Christian has been clearly brought out, not until the heresy of efficiency has been overcome, can human life breathe liberty, can it be filled with sovereign greatness. In this primacy lies the extreme antithesis to the "bourgeois," to a narrowing pettiness, to every possible enslavement in one's profession. *This* life is royal, whatever one's profession may be, because he who lives it can say: "What can separate me from the love of Christ?"